Brian Freemantle is a journalist and novelist who lives in London. He is a former foreign correspondent for the *Daily Express* and Foreign Editor for the *Daily Mail*. He has worked in more than thirty countries, including the U.S.S.R., U.S.A. and Vietnam. His books have been published in a total of thirteen countries.

BRIAN FREEMANTLE

KGB

Futura
Macdonald & Co
London & Sydney

A Futura Book

Dedication
To Emma and Charlotte

Copyright © Innslodge Publications Ltd 1982

First published in Great Britain in 1983
by Michael Joseph Ltd and
The Rainbird Publishing Group Ltd

This edition published in 1984 by
Futura Publications
a Division of
Macdonald & Co (Publishers) Ltd
London & Sydney

ISBN 0 7088 2503 6

Reproduced, printed and bound in Great Britain by
Hazell Watson & Viney Limited
Member of the BPCC Group
Aylesbury, Bucks

Futura Publications
A Division of
Macdonald & Co (Publishers) Ltd
Maxwell House
74 Worship Street
London EC2A 2EN
A BPCC plc Company

CONTENTS

AUTHOR'S ACKNOWLEDGMENTS

Some of the people who helped me with this book have to lead anonymous lives and so my appreciation of their guidance must be anonymous: it is none the less sincere, particularly to a courtly man with whom I took coffee in an English south- coast county and another, equally courteous, whom I met in a suburb of Washington.

Others can be named.

I owe particular gratitude to Mrs Annabel Markov.

Thanks are due to Tom Kelly and the staff of the *Daily Mail* library in England. To Jay Melvin and the *Newsweek* organization in New York. There, too, Dudley Freeman, for whom sufficient gratitude will always be difficult. In Washington, William Lowther and Angus Macpherson. Ms Ratri Banerjee helped more than she knew and Bill Cromaitie made the index of the Library of Congress far easier than I would initially have found it. The staff at the Senate and House libraries showed a willingness to help that makes researching in America such a delight. And Bruce Wilson and Ross Mark were friends.

To them all – the named and the unnamed – I acknowledge my deep appreciation.

Winchester 1981

Author's Note
This book was written for simultaneous publication in England and the United States. Monetary sums have therefore been printed in both English and U.S. currencies at the conversion rate relevant to the year of such expenditure.

There is a glossary of the more unusual English terms and Russian words used in the language of spying on page 185.

CHAPTER ONE

THE ASSASSINATION OF AN IRRITATING DISSIDENT

The relationship was the attraction of opposites, Georgi Markov, the brilliant intellectual playwright and novelist with the fitting workers' background, and Todor Zhivkov, the peasant-born Communist Party leader of Bulgaria.

Markov's plays and books – *The Cheese Merchant's Good Lady*, *Portrait of My Double*, *The Women of Warsaw* – were officially approved and praised: even, cautiously, permitted to criticize some of the failings within the country.

Markov was accepted. And being accepted, he was admitted to the inner, favoured circle of the government leaders. There were visits to Zhivkov's country retreat at Mount Vitosha, the sealed-off, guarded sanctuary of the party hierarchy. Here, among the pines and the mountain streams, clear enough to drink from, they have their cabins. It is hunting country but Markov did not hunt. Instead, he walked and talked, learning the reality of the life of the communist élite.

He witnessed the chauffeur-driven cars on errand-ready standby, the kitchens and the refrigerators stocked with Western food and drink unknown in the sparse shop windows of Sofia. And he listened, realizing that people as well as commodities could be bought during sealed-envelope meetings at recognized restaurants. And he remembered.

In 1968, the frail-looking Alexander Dubček made his brave but pitiful attempt to liberalize Czechoslovakia from its crushing Soviet domination. The Russian response was as it had been in Hungary, twelve years earlier. But more than Czech hopes were crushed under the tracks of Soviet tanks. The order to halt and reverse any indication of liberalization went from Moscow to all its satellites.

Bulgaria is the most dutiful of communist acolytes; Markov was later to describe the relationship between Moscow and

Sofia as being similar to that of an English lord and his indispensable butler. Zhivkov's response to the Russian order was immediate and absolute. Georgi Markov was no longer welcome at Mount Vitosha. Nor was he permitted to write the plays of the past. And certainly not the most recent sort, a comment upon the contemporary life in Bulgaria which so incensed the newly programmed and corrected Zhivkov that he personally wrote a savage critique of it in a Sofia newspaper.

Markov defected. He knew the risks he was taking. To defect, famous as he was, constituted a crime sufficient to earn him a six-and-a-half-year jail sentence *in absentia*. For the defector to have been a friend of Zhivkov and his ministers – and worse, a confidant and witness of the good life at Mount Vitosha – elevated the crime to a personal and insulting level.

But Markov did not stop there. After a brief pause in Italy, where his defector brother Nikola was domiciled, he travelled to London and became a programme assistant in the Bulgarian section of the British Broadcasting Corporation's External Service. From the BBC's vast, labyrinthine Bush House, on its triangular island between London's Strand and Fleet Street, he began broadcasting on their thrice daily service beamed to his homeland. It was a cautious, subdued start; he read the news – as he continued to do throughout his employment by the BBC – and he wrote a weekly cultural programme.

He met, fell in love with and married Annabel, daughter of Christopher Dilke, one-time head of the BBC's English-by-Radio service. They lived in Lynette Avenue, in the London suburb of Clapham. They had a daughter, Sasha. Markov began writing again for London's fringe theatre; his themes were critical of Bulgaria.

In 1977 Markov's father, an army officer, became terminally ill in Sofia. Markov and his brother appealed to the Bulgarian embassy in Rome for their parents to be allowed out of Bulgaria. Their mother was permitted a visit later in the year, but their father was not. He died, so Markov never saw his father again.

To Markov's dispassionate contempt of the hypocrisy of the

Bulgarian communist leadership was now added a personal bitterness. He recalled the close-curtained limousine rides to Mount Vitosha and the conversations with Zhivkov and his ministers. And he began disclosing details of those sybaritic weekends in his memoirs broadcast from the Munich headquarters of Radio Free Europe, which had been broadcasting his work since 1975. The memoirs, transmitted over a period of two years, were called *In Absentia Reports about Bulgaria*. In June 1978, he broadcast *A Letter to My Father*. His programmes exposed the cant of the political indoctrination that is a feature of Bulgarian working life. He knew it well. Markov had at one time been in charge of an engineering factory.

From exile this chemical engineer-turned-writer achieved an audience as great, if not greater, than he could have hoped from his plays had he remained in Sofia; Annabel estimates that his listening public numbered 5,000,000 in a country of 8,000,000 people. The Darjavna Sigurnost, the Bulgarian secret police, tried to jam the broadcasts. Illogically they left a channel open to monitor the programmes for themselves. The Bulgarian public discovered the free channel; and Georgi Markov's audience did not diminish.

To Bulgaria – and to its Moscow controllers – Markov's betrayal was complete. For the factual accounts of Bulgarian life were being transmitted over a radio service which had, until 1971, been admittedly funded by the American Central Intelligence Agency. From 1973, to diminish accusations of blatant propagandizing, the funding was taken over by the U.S. Congress – appointed public board. Not even Washington – and certainly not Moscow – believed different accountants affected the control of Radio Free Europe.

One section of the *Absentia* reports was sub-titled *Meetings with Todor Zhivkov*. In the broadcasts, Markov disclosed Zhivkov's involvement in and apparent encouragement of the cultural life in Bulgaria, an involvement which was a sham to enable him to have complete control and manipulation of it. Markov said, 'In my opinion no one else in Bulgaria has exerted a more devastating, destructive influence over the life of the artistic intelligentsia.' He claimed that Communist Party interference was absolute, adding, 'And behind this interference as its chief organizer and conductor stood Todor Zhivkov. No more nor less important action affecting the life of the artistic intelligentsia, no serious appointment or dismissal, no punishment or reward could take place over the head of the First Secretary. . . . Under his immediate direction real assaults took place against important cultural organizations and institutions.' Zhivkov was enraged by these broadcasts and so was Moscow.

Markov was warned that he might be murdered, first in a telephone call and then by a visit to Clapham from a Bulgarian. Annabel is still unsure whether the man, whom she will not identify, was a friend or an enemy. Georgi was frightened – he had always known the danger, from the moment he fled to Italy – but he did not stop writing for Radio Free Europe or the German service transmitted to Bulgaria, Deutsche Welle. Annabel recalls that neither of them fully believed an assassination attempt would really be made: cold-blooded liquidation was the stuff of spy fiction, make-believe outside the limits of credibility. Markov, however, was still careful. Annabel says he never entered dark alleys or unlit streets. Having gained the impression that his death would be attempted from some poison administered orally, he was cautious of everything he ate and drank. The Markov's telephone was ex-directory. Their friends included Bulgarian émigrés – as Georgi was – but they were always cautious when a new face entered the group.

On Thursday, 7 September 1978, it was Markov's turn for the dog-watch duty, a twelve-hour tour at Bush House with only a brief break between the night-time transmission on the Bulgarian service and the early-morning broadcast. By September, Markov – handsomely white-haired, six-feet tall and weighing nearly fourteen stone – had begun to relax the caution that he had exercised following the assassination warning at the beginning of the year. It had become a recent habit most days to park the green and cream Simca van in which he drove from Clapham in a side street on the south side of the Thames, near the South Bank complex. Then at 6.30 p.m. he would leave the BBC building – after reading the evening news – to walk the half mile across Waterloo Bridge and move the vehicle conveniently nearer to Bush

House when the parking restrictions were lifted at the end of the day.

That September day there had been a forecast of rain and a few scattered showers, but it was fine when he left the huge white building bracketed at either end like book markers by the Citibank and the Australian High Commission. There were still many people about with raincoats and still more with umbrellas.

There are bus stops at either end of Waterloo Bridge – near the underpass into Holborn to the north and near the National Theatre and the Festival Hall to the south. Markov had just passed the queue near the National Theatre when he felt a sharp thrust against his right thigh.

Almost immediately there was a short, burning pain. Markov's turning caused an umbrella to twist out of the hand of the man facing him, apparently waiting in a bus queue. The man apologized, in English, but with a foreign accent. Seeming confused, he snatched the umbrella up, hailed a passing taxi showing a yellow 'For Hire' sign and drove off. The pain in Markov's thigh had been momentary: he did nothing to stop the man. He did not speak to him.

It was past 7 p.m. when Markov arrived back at Bush House after collecting his van. In the office of the Bulgarian section he told a fellow exile, Teo Lirkoff, that he had been stabbed by an assailant with an umbrella. He took his jeans down and they found a small, angry red mark on his thigh. It looked like an insect bite.

Markov arrived back home in Lynette Avenue at about 10.30 p.m. and went to sleep on a bed set up in his study, to avoid disturbing Annabel when he got up for the dawn shift back at Bush House. But she was disturbed and heard him moving around at about 2 a.m. She discovered that he had been sick and his temperature was 104°F. Their doctor, whom she telephoned, said it was probably influenza: there was a lot of it about at the time.

Annabel sat up with her husband. Suddenly he said, 'I have a horrible suspicion that it might be connected with something that happened today.' When she asked what he meant, he told her about the umbrella attack.

His condition deteriorated so rapidly that he was admitted

to St James's Hospital, in the London district of Balham. He went into shock and was put at once into intensive care. The surgeons were baffled by Markov's illness. There was an abnormally high fever, with indications of a septaecemia from some 'very toxic' substance. His white blood count rose to 33,000 per cubic millimetre, the highest physicians there had ever encountered; the normal count ranges between 5,000 and 10,000. There were times when Markov, in his delirium, was violent but there were other moments of rational clarity. During one of these recoveries, he recounted again his experience on Waterloo Bridge. An X-ray of the red puncture mark on his thigh indicated something of a high metallic density.

On Monday, 11 September, Georgi Markov died. The cause of his poisoning could not be determined by surgeons and consultants. From Markov's thigh was recovered a minute metal ball, 1.52 millimetres in diameter. It was made of almost 90 per cent platinum and 10 per cent iridium, with minuscule traces of rhodium and palladium. It would have fitted the tip of an umbrella. In it were bored two pintip holes, 0.35 millimetres wide; originally they had been sealed by wax which had been melted by Markov's body heat, to release the contents of the tiny pellet.

The ball – and tissue samples from Markov's body – were subjected to analysis at the top-secret British Government Chemical Defence establishment at Porton Down, in Wiltshire. There, scientists identified what had been inside the hollowed ball, the poison that killed Georgi Markov.

It was ricin, a protein derivative of the castor oil plant and ranked – along with botulinus, diphtheria, tetanus and gramicidin – as one of the five most toxic elements in the world. Twice as strong as cobra venom, one gram of ricin is sufficient to kill 36,000 people. At Porton Down there was medical suspicion that to increase its potency before it was administered to Markov, the ricin had been mixed with some anaerobic bacteria of the sort that creates gangrene.

During both world wars ricin – under the codeletter *W* – was considered by British chemical warfare planners as the most effective mass poison with which to attack an enemy. There are two countries in which ricin is included in continuing research. One is Czechoslovakia and the other is Hungary. Both are communist, controlled by the Soviet Union. Russia is the major producer of the metals used to make the ricin pellet.

At the inquest into the death of Georgi Markov on 2 January 1979, the verdict was returned that he was 'killed unlawfully'. By grotesque irony Markov's last play in Bulgaria – the play which drove Zhivkov into critical print – was called *The Assassin*.

Officially, investigation continues into the murder of Georgi Markov. But after three years, his assassin remains undetected. He was a professional. He worked under the instructions of the KGB.

CHAPTER TWO

THE HISTORY OF THE KGB

Contrary to the later attempts of Soviet historians to make it appear otherwise, the Bolshevik revolution of October 1917 was not a spontaneous, countrywide uprising of the welcoming Russian peasantry and proletariat. It was a daring, second attempt at a *coup d'état* conducted with political skill by Lenin and Trotsky who for twelve years had waited patiently for their opportunity. And once had got it wrong.

It was in 1905 that the first cracks openly appeared in the three-hundred-year old almost-mystical but absolute rule of the Romanov family. A year earlier Russia had clashed in an undeclared war with Japan over conflicting attempts to expand into Manchuria and Korea. At the hands of a minuscule nation, mighty Russia suffered ignominious defeat after defeat. Humiliation abroad was unbearable. With the unbearable came the unacceptable: internal dissent, from a over-taxed, oppressed peasantry and emerging workforce.

A weak, prevaricating man, Tsar Nicholas II gave an undertaking – which he initially had little intention of carrying through – to establish a constitutional assembly. For a population which had never known anything but despotic, autocratic rule, the concession did not allay unrest. Paradoxically, unrest increased: if one concession was to be allowed, then others could be achieved. Throughout 1905, until September, when America mediated a peace settlement of the Japanese war, Russia was wracked by strikes and assassinations. In June, sailors aboard the *Potemkin*, a battleship of the Black Sea Fleet, mutinied and for a while there was a risk of the rebellion spreading to the rest of the navy and the army as well. For the last ten days of October, European Russia was paralysed by a general strike. On 30 October, the Tsar was forced to keep his promise. He established a government, the Duma, but still attempted to make it his puppet, reserving the right to legislate by decree and limiting its financial powers.

The Tsar considered his strength the other method of

control: his secret security organization. Under the Ministry of the Interior existed the Department of State Police, formed in 1880, which consisted of a central, special department, the *Osobyi Otdel* and throughout the country a web of security divisions, *Okhrannye Otdeleniya*. To the population, the hated, oppressive network was known simply as Okhrana.

Through the Okhrana, the Tsar attempted to infiltrate and neutralize the various revolutionary movements threatening his throne. With a surprisingly small staff – in 1916, it numbered little more than 15,000 – it was amazingly successful. Ironically its major achievements were within the Bolshevik Party, ultimately to replace the Tsar as Russia's ruler. Lenin, the school inspector's son turned revolutionary, had to flee to Switzerland from the Okhrana in 1906. He left Roman Malinovskii behind as his main spokesman in Russia. A member of the Bolshevik Central Committee, Malinovskii was a dedicated Okhrana agent. When *Pravda* was founded in St Petersburg in 1912, Malinovskii became its editor. Between 1908 and 1909, four of the five members of the St Petersburg committee of the Bolshevik Party were Okhrana officials.

As well as infiltration there were purges. Hundreds of suspected dissidents were arrested. Some were jailed, others liquidated.

There were four Dumas and during the government of the second and third some basic reforms were achieved. Then, in 1914, Russia was brought into World War I on the side of the Allies. In two and a half years, the Russians suffered 5,500,000 casualties. Soldiers had no bullets and the population no food. The transport system sank into chaos. The fourth Duma splintered into squabbling factions; in the last twelve months there were four prime ministers, three war ministers and three foreign ministers.

In November 1916, the final collapsing government warned the Tsar that unless he agreed to changes in the regime there was a risk of revolution. Satisfied that his Okhrana agents were placed within every insurrectionist movement, the Tsar ignored them.

Three months later, housewives queuing for bread in what had been St Petersburg but which had, in 1914, been renamed Petrograd, suddenly staged brush-fire protests. Within days 400,000 industrial workers went on strike. The February uprising *was* spontaneous and because not one of the revolutionary parties was involved, the Tsar and the Okhrana were completely unprepared. After five days of work stoppages and marches throughout Petrograd, the army garrison mutinied, siding with the civil population.

One month later, the Provisional Committee of the State Duma became the Provisional Government. Two days after its formation, the Tsar abdicated.

The Petrograd provisional government established, for a brief nine months, the only democracy Russia has ever known. They announced complete and immediate amnesty for political prisoners. They declared freedom of speech and press, and the right to gather for meetings. To strike would be legal. A government would be elected by secret ballot.

Perhaps its most important edict was to abolish the secret police: to escape lynching, members of the Okhrana queued for arrest at the Tauride Palace, the seat of government.

In Berlin, the overthrow of the Tsar was seen as a major opportunity to split the Allies and to take Russia out of the war. The German General Staff provided a special sealed train in which Lenin was carried across Europe to Petrograd: the expectation was that Lenin and his Bolsheviks would foment disaffection among Soviet troops which would lead to a collapse on the Eastern front. There were widespread desertions – by the time of the October revolution, more than two million men had fled the battlefront – but these had little to do with Lenin's persuasion. His concentration was centred upon gaining power. He arrived in Petrograd on 16 April and for three months planned his coup. He attempted it on 18 July and failed. Once again Lenin was forced to flee – this time to Poland and Finland. A month later General Kornilov attempted a military take-over of the government headed by the prime minister, Aleksandr Kerensky (whose schoolmaster father had taught Lenin at Simbirsk). The military take-over failed – the Bolshevik Red Guard fought against them – but showed further the disarray into which the provisional government, ineffectually backed by a people's militia in place of police and without the support of the army, had fallen.

Secretly Lenin returned to Petrograd. Throughout the month of September the Bolsheviks worked to attain a majority in the Petrograd Soviet. They increased, too, their influence throughout the country.

On 10 October a clandestine meeting of the Bolshevik Party Central Committee took place. A resolution of which Lenin was the author was put before the Committee. It said: 'An armed rising is inevitable and the time perfectly ripe.'

Two days later the government formed a Military Revolutionary Committee, allegedly for the defence of Petrograd against the advance of German troops. The Bolsheviks controlled it. Commissars were posted to every military unit within the city to guarantee support for the coup. Supporting the committee was the Red Guard – factory workers formed into armed units.

The Military Revolutionary Committee had its headquarters at the Smolny Institute, which was also the headquarters of the Petrograd Soviet. The provisional government was at the Winter Palace and its cabinet was meeting during the night of 25 October. At midnight, the Military Committee stormed the palace, seizing the government with little fighting. Kerensky escaped, to mount a short-lived, abortive resistance.

Lenin made a proclamation after the coup. It said: 'To the citizens of Russia! The provisional government is deposed. State power has passed into the hands of the organ of the Petrograd Soviet of Workers' and Soldiers' Deputies – the Military Revolutionary Committee which stands at the head of the Petrograd proletariat and garrison.' Lenin at last had power. He was determined to keep it. He knew the way.

The security of the Smolny Institute, a classically fronted building originally a finishing school for the daughters of the St Petersburg nobility, was essential during the planning of the October coup. It was entrusted to a goatee-bearded, nervously intense Polish nobleman who had been a victim of the Tsarist Okhrana and an inmate of their prisons. His name was Feliks Edmundovich Dzerzhinsky.

Dzerzhinsky was a revolutionary fanatic whose first ambition had been to become a Roman Catholic priest. Already his health was suffering from his periods of imprisonment: in jail he contracted tuberculosis from which he never fully recovered, despite enforced periods of treatment in Switzerland after the October revolution and at the Polish resort of Zakopane. Utterly humourless, this multilingual man – he spoke Polish, Russian, English and Yiddish – committed himself absolutely to the cause of Bolshevism. Within a month of the revolution, his proposal to establish a Commission for Combatting Counter-Revolution and Sabotage was accepted by the Military Revolutionary Council. Drunkenness swept the city, as law and order collapsed and the houses and palaces of the rich were looted by hooligans. At Dzerzhinsky's suggestion, the wine in the cellars of the Winter Palace was poured into the river Neva and all other stores of alcohol were destroyed. A People's Commissariat for Internal Affairs – the NKVD – was established and ordered to create a militia. Dzerzhinsky was a member of the collegium from the start. Under Dzerzhinsky's chairmanship, the Military Revolutionary Committee investigated various counter-insurrectionary movements. On 5 December 1917, the Military Revolutionary Committee declared its own dissolution, handing its responsibilities – in reality maintaining the Bolsheviks in power – to the appropriate department of the All Russian Central Executive Committee, the *Vserossiiskii Tsentralnyi Ispolnitelnyi Komitet*. The only department answering that function was the counter-revolution and sabotage commission established upon Dzerzhinsky's suggestion. Before there could be a formal decision, the Council of People's Commissars, the *Sovet Narodnykh Komissarov* received information about a general strike throughout the country. Dzerzhinsky, at Lenin's urging, was charged with stopping it.

Dzerzhinsky told the Central Executive Committee: 'It is war now – face to face, a fight to the finish. Life or death! I propose, I demand, an organ for the revolutionary settlement of accounts with counter-revolutionaries. And we must act not tomorrow, but today.' It did act that very same day.

On 20 December 1917, the committee resolved to form the Vecheka, the All Russian Extraordinary Commission (for Combatting Counter-Revolution, Speculation, Sabotage and

Misconduct in Office), the *Vserossiiskaya Chrezvychainaya Komissiya (po borbe s Kontrrevolyutsiei Spekuliatsiei, Sabotazhem i Prestupleniyami po Dolzhnosti)*. Thus was formed – not by the legal basis of decree but simply by resolution – what is today the KGB. By calling it 'extraordinary', the inference was that it was to be temporary.

Lenin was a believer in terror and a fervent admirer of the Jacobins, the most radical of the French revolutionaries of 1790. The day before the resolution to form the Vecheka – almost immediately shortened to *Cheka* which in Russian means lynchpin – Lenin described the character necessary for its chairman. 'We must' he said, 'find a staunch proletarian Jacobin.'

Despite his aristocratic origins, Dzerzhinsky was the unanimous choice. Only ten months earlier – in March 1917 – the February revolution had freed him from the Butyrki jail in Moscow, where he had been imprisoned since 1912, serving a sentence for terrorist activities. Now aged forty, he had spent eleven years of his life – three doing hard labour – in prison or in Siberian exile. Since February, he had been intimately involved in secret plans to bring the Bolsheviks to power. Now they were in power; and no uncertain revolution, riven by internal crime, food shortages, civil war and an external conflict with Germany, could have had a better man to safeguard its security.

After preliminary meetings at the Smolny Institute, Dzerzhinsky created the first headquarters of the Russian security service. It was at 2, Gorokhovaia Street in Petrograd. Today it is known as Dzerzhinsky Street. After the ratification of the Brest-Litovsk peace treaty with Germany in March 1918, the Bolsheviks moved their government from Petrograd to Moscow. Dzerzhinsky and the Cheka hierarchy went with them. On 30 March they established their headquarters at Bolshoi Lubyanka 11, close to the Kremlin. Here they were to remain for over two years before moving, in December 1920, to their present site, formerly the offices of the All Russian Insurance Company.

The growth of the Cheka – creating the skeleton upon which the Frankenstein of today's KGB has been moulded – was startling. What began simply as an investigative body quickly expanded, with Lenin's active encouragement, to have powers of summary arrest, trial and execution. It was vested with powers to incarcerate in concentration camps. During the civil war which raged until 1920, it frequently took hostages of other revolutionary parties to ensure the loyalty of those remaining free.

Protesters came up against Lenin's philosophy: 'We have hundreds of LSRs [Left Socialist Revolutionaries] as hostages. We must mercilessly crush everywhere these miserable and hysterical adventurers who have become weapons in the hands of the counter-revolutionaries.'

In the food-growing areas, twenty or thirty hostages were selected from among the wealthier inhabitants; if the excess food was not delivered for distribution to combat the growing famine, they were shot. This initial development of the Russian security apparatus – during which 500,000 people died – became known as the Red Terror. The name has changed but the process has not.

A man who controlled thugs, Dzerzhinsky was not a thug himself. Although he denied it, he was politically astute. In 1919 he succeeded in being appointed to a commissar's position with the NKVD, thus removing any threat of take-over by the Interior Ministry. Almost at once he began merging parallel departments, with the Cheka appointees taking control.

The number of people murdered or imprisoned was numerically greater during Stalin's reign, but under Lenin's prompting and Dzerzhinsky's enthusiastic obedience, hundreds of thousands of Russians either perished or were incarcerated. Dzerzhinsky declared: 'We terrorize the enemies of the Soviet Government in order to stifle crime at its inception.' By 1920 that policy had become unacceptable, particularly to the outside world with whom Lenin was anxious to establish economic relations, and internally where the word Cheka was synonymous with terror.

Once again Dzerzhinsky showed his political ability, recognizing that a blemish on the face of revolution needed cosmetic treatment. With the ending of the civil war – although not the civil unrest – in November 1920, the more obvious need for the Cheka ceased to exist. Dzerzhinsky himself suggested reform. It took a year for this to evolve.

In January 1922, the hated name Cheka was abandoned and replaced by GPU, the *Gosudarstvennoe Politicheskoe Upravlenie* or State Political Administration. Further, the Politburo decided it should be integrated completely with the NKVD. Reforms were decreed, limiting the *carte blanche* powers the Cheka had managed to obtain for itself. Throughout the Cheka structure, new titles and names were created: in practice, the departments and divisions remained largely unchanged. Dzerzhinsky remained as chairman.

Within two months, in secret correspondence, Lenin was complaining about the relaxation of terror. In a letter concerning the formulation of a Criminal Code, he wrote, 'The law should not abolish terror: to promise that would be self-delusion or deception; it should be substantiated and legalized in principle, clearly, without evasion or embellishment. The paragraph on terror should be formulated as widely as possible, since only revolutionary consciousness of justice and revolutionary conscious can determine the conditions of its application in practice.'

By August the GPU had regained the Cheka right to sentence, without any judicial hearing, a counter-revolutionary to exile for a period not exceeding three years. The term counter-revolutionary had a wide application. By October, for banditry, they were authorized summarily to punish and even execute criminals caught at the scene of their crime. The term banditry had wide application.

The pruning of the Cheka personnel had not diminished the GPU effectiveness. There is an estimate that by 1921-2, one in every four city dwellers was a secret informant. Under Dzerzhinsky's continued control the GPU regained virtually all the power it had enjoyed as the Cheka. By 1923, it was even extending it. Dzerzhinsky chaired a Central Committee sub-committee examining internal problems within the party and the recommendation was that any evidence concerning dissent within the party should be reported to the GPU as well as to the Central Committee, thus creating the precedent of party members informing upon other party members that still exists in the Soviet Union today.

In 1923, the security system of Russia underwent a third name change. In July of that year there was adopted a constitution of the Union of Soviet Socialist Republics. It was necessary for such an important arm of Russian government to be given a national and not a republican title. Thus the GPU became the OGPU – Unified State Political Administration – which meant it was responsible directly in Moscow to the Central Committee; in the republics, the working arm remained the GPU. Once more, Feliks Dzerzhinsky remained chairman of the OGPU, *Obedinennoe Gosudarstvennoe Politicheskoe Upravlenye*.

In May 1922, Lenin suffered the first of his three incapacitating strokes. Even before this Dzerzhinsky and Lenin had argued over policy differences and there is evidence that Lenin intended purging Dzerzhinsky, just as he tried, in his will, to prevent power after his death falling into the hands of Joseph Stalin. Lenin's third stroke, in March 1923, prevented his achieving either. He lived for a further ten months, dying in January 1924.

Dzerzhinsky arranged Lenin's funeral. Although the title does not fit, the axiom 'the king is dead: long live the king' is appropriate. Within a short time, on 24 February 1924, Stalin appointed Dzerzhinsky controller of the Soviet Union's economic programme – while retaining him as chairman of the OGPU. Under the influence of his new protector, Dzerzhinsky entered the Politburo as a candidate member. When the battle for succession was fought out between Stalin and Trotsky, after Lenin's death, Dzerzhinsky sided with Stalin who won. It was fitting, therefore, that after Khrushchev's denunciation of Stalin at the 20th Party Congress and the removal of Stalin's body from its place of honour in the Lenin Mausoleum, his remains were re-interred next to Dzerzhinsky's in the Kremlin wall.

During the last two years of Dzerzhinsky's life – he died in 1926, still chairman of the State's security organization – he provided the necessary, constant support for Stalin whose political victory was initially an uncertain one. He faced powerful opposition from Rightist members within the Politburo. Chief among these was Nikolai Bukharin, who made the accusation openly to the Politburo that their rule was being replaced by a Stalin dictatorship. It took the devious Stalin until 1929 to rout that opposition. Having succeeded, he then embarked upon the first terror campaign of his regime, a scheme that was to open the catalogue upon the millions of deaths for which he was responsible.

In its early years, the fragile base of the Bolshevik revolution had almost foundered under Lenin's attempts to establish absolute state control of the economy. Lenin had retreated, evolving instead a programme known as the New Economic Policy. Under this policy had prospered kulaks – peasants who remained independent and became rich, establishing themselves in turn as the employers of other peasants. Under this independent system, agriculture had been moderately successful. But insufficient surplus was being produced either for export – to earn foreign currency with which to purchase machinery – or to provide the major cities; in provincial towns bread rationing was introduced in 1928 and in Moscow and Leningrad at the beginning of 1929.

Stalin, who had no economic experience or knowledge, introduced the policy of collectivization. This meant that Russian agriculture was to come under the control of the state and its efficiency improved under state administration. There was the additional advantage that it put under state – and therefore security – control an independent group of people who might sometime consider counter-revolution. Originally the change from private to state-ownership was scheduled to take place within five years. Stalin ordered this to be reduced to one year: but later this had to be extended.

Stalin entrusted the campaign of terror, aimed at making his programme work, to Dzerzhinsky's successor and previously his deputy, Vyacheslav Rudolfich Menzhinsky. Like Dzerzhinsky, Menzhinsky was a Pole. Between January and March 1930, fourteen million peasant holdings – half the total in the entire country – were turned into collectives. The peasants rebelled almost to the point of another civil war, destroying livestock and physically trying to fight off Menzhinsky's OGPU with guns, axes and knives. Had the political opposition to Stalin been more organized, it is possible that he could have been toppled. But it was fragmented. Stalin urged the OGPU to greater, crushing efforts, ordering grain and milk to be forcibly removed from farms to meet export targets. The result was an OGPU-created famine. The disaster has never officially or fully been admitted, but it is estimated that 5,500,000 people died from hunger or hunger-related illnesses. The OGPU conceded in a report to Stalin a figure of 3,500,000 deaths.

By 1934 Stalin had decided he wanted to take the Soviet Union into the League of Nations and realized, once again, that the bloodthirsty reputation of the OGPU in the West made its continuation unacceptable. It was time for another cosmetic renaming. Plans were already underway when Menzhinsky died. He was replaced by Genrikh Grigorevich Yagoda, who had proved his ability in the terror organization by running the administrative arm of the peasant-slaughtering apparatus. Yagoda was a trained pharmacist and under his chairmanship the Russian security service greatly expanded its laboratory facilities and research into scientific methods of extermination. Yagoda himself liked to conduct human experiments in the cells below Lubyanka. He had a poison chest which he carried with him from his office. When – inevitably under Stalin's reign – Yagoda was purged and stood trial, he confessed to using the poison chest to kill the writer Maxim Gorky and the man whom he himself succeeded, Vyacheslav Menzhinsky.

The OGPU became a directorate of the NKVD, the *Narodnyi Komissariat Vnutrennikh Del*. So, too, did most of the sections of the Comintern, the Communist International, the intelligence organization by which the Russians were attempting to influence other countries. This was the time of their greatest success. There was still the romanticism about the revolution which appealed to the intellectuals of the West. It was during this period – when the Comintern was staffed not predominantly by Russians but by intellectual East Europeans – that the Russian infiltration of the British universities of Oxford and Cambridge resulted in the recruitment of people such as Anthony Blunt, Guy Burgess, Kim Philby and Donald Maclean, with the later, disastrous consequences for British intelligence.

Internally, Stalin was building up to the time of the Great Terror, the period of show trials, mass extermination and concentration and labour-camp incarcerations which, by conservative estimates, took the lives of ten million people. In

October 1935, a special department for state security, known as *Upravlenie Gosudarstvennoe Bezopasnosti*, was added to the NKVD. For eight months this new department was under the control of Nikolai Ivanovich Yezhov, secretary of the Central Committee. Then, in June 1936, Yagoda was purged, put on show trial as a murderer and foreign spy and shot in the cells of Lubyanka where he had conducted his own poison experiments. Yezhov assumed absolute control.

Terror within Russia reached its height under Yezhov, to the degree that the exterminations that took place during this time are collectively referred to as *Yezhovshchina*. A diminutive man, not quite five-feet tall, Yezhov was known as 'the bloody dwarf'. No one was safe during his rule: in 1937, three thousand NKVD men – his own workers – were executed. Within two years, Stalin realized that Yezhov knew more than anyone else about the genocide that was being committed within the country. It was far too dangerous to stage a show trial so Yezhov was purged in December 1938, and shot in the cell adjoining that in which Yagoda had been killed.

His successor, in December 1938, was Lavrenti Pavlovich Beria who had joined the Cheka under Dzerzhinsky's leadership. His recommendation to Dzerzhinsky had come from Stalin. Stalin wrote, 'He is a brilliant young comrade, who has done excellent work among the oil workers of Baku. I consider him fully trustworthy and well fitted to serve [in the Vecheka].'

Upon Stalin's death, in 1953, Beria, with the secret-service empire he had created during his fifteen-year chairmanship, came within a hair's breadth of establishing himself as outright dictator.

Beria, like Stalin, was a Georgian, having been born in Tiflis. His father was a civil servant and Beria's ambition was to be an architect. After attending a teacher's training college, he entered the Tsarist army. Beria's *pince-nez* perched precariously on the bridge of his nose is a familiar feature of almost every photograph of the man; his poor eyesight prevented him being sent to the battlefront. Beria frequently boasted a history as an early revolutionary, inciting soldiers to mutiny and then escaping to join Georgian rebels – whose leader he became in 1917 – after a court-martial sentence of death. There is little factual evidence to support this. Certainly he had to flee when the White Russian Army defeated the revolutionaries and gained control of the Caucasus. Under the assumed name of Vanno Daheshvili he hid at Omsk, in Siberia, where he established a friendship with a recently released Croat prisoner of war, Josip Broz, later to become Yugoslavia's Marshal Tito. Beria's first employment with the Cheka was as an illegal agent abroad. He spoke fluent French, German and Czech and worked in Prague and Paris, infiltrating émigré groups. It was Beria who trailed Trotsky from Turkey to Germany, to Denmark and finally to Mexican assassination after Trotsky failed to win the leadership battle with Stalin. Beria was a brilliant if ambitious secret service chief and during World War II organized some exceptional intelligence coups for his country. That they were not properly utilized was due to Stalin's frequent refusal to believe the information he received.

At the height of the war Beria had expanded his empire into almost unmanageable proportions. The NKVD virtually governed Siberia and through its forced labour camps was in charge of a large section of Soviet industry. In order to manage this empire more efficiently, it was decided to transfer the security apparatus into a separate organization. The new name was NKGB, *Narodnyi Komissariat Gosudarstvennoe Bezopasnosti*. The division of responsibility put the NKVD in charge of police administration, the secret service and civil administration. The NKGB was entrusted with internal security, counter-espionage, frontier guards, administration of corrective labour camps and guerrilla and underground activities against the Germans.

Beria remained chairman of the NKVD but the division did not mean any diminution of his control as the man who headed the NKGB, Vsevolod Nikolaevich Merkulov, was one of his henchmen.

After the war, both the NKGB and the NKVD were elevated to ministries. The NKGB became the MGB, *Ministerstvo Gosudarstvennoe Bezopasnosti*, responsible for state security. The NKVD was renamed MVD, *Ministerstvo Vnutrennikh Del*, in charge of internal affairs. As deputy chairman of the council of ministers — effectively deputy premier – Beria retained overall control. Sergey Nikoforovich Kruglov was appointed controller of the MVD and Merkulov stayed in charge of the MGB. In 1950 Merkulov was replaced by General Viktor Semonovich Abakumov who during the war had headed a department dear to the hearts of all James Bond lovers, SMERSH, an acronym of the Russian words *smert shpionam*, which translates as 'death to spies'.

Abakumov had no allegiance to Beria. Worse, Stalin created a Committee of Information which took over control of external intelligence formerly under the aegis of the MGB. It absorbed, too, the GRU, the *Glavnoe Razvedyvatelnoe Upravlenie*, the Chief Intelligence Directorate of the Soviet General Staff.

Briefly – Beria later purged the army and earned its hatred as a result – the military and Beria joined forces to regain control. The army recovered the GRU within a year. Beria framed Abakumov, convincing the ever-paranoid Stalin of a plot. Abakumov – like Merkulov – was shot in Lubyanka and the MGB took back its overseas control. Semen Denisovich Ignatiev was appointed director. Ignatiev and Kruglov were obedient and Beria was content.

When Stalin died in March 1953, Beria saw his chance of gaining supreme power within the Soviet Union. Ignatiev and Kruglov were deposed and Beria merged the MVD and MGB, taking overall control. Beria's power was enormous: he commanded the political police, the external espionage activities; the militia and 300,000 troops were his; the labour camps and their inmates were under his direction, meaning that he was responsible for a substantial portion of Russian industry.

For two months, it looked as if the axiom that had applied at Lenin's death, 'the king is dead, long live the king', might be repeated. But Beria had underestimated Stalin's acolyte, Georgi Malenkov. He was overly dismissive too of Khrushchev and Vyacheslav Molotov. And the army had not forgiven him for purging some of their better generals. Malenkov had already made an arrangement with the army. Marshal Ivan Konev presided at Beria's trial. Beria died – as other security chiefs had done before him – in front of a firing squad in Lubyanka.

The take-over of one dictatorship by another had almost succeeded. The Soviet Politburo determined that never again would the state security organization be allowed to grow unfettered as it had under Beria. Sweeping changes were introduced, the most important of which was to make it answerable directly to the Politburo. Its functions – control of police, clandestine operations, border patrols and internal security – were strictly defined. The industrial responsibilities were distributed among other ministries. The right of summary trial and sentence was taken over by the Ministry of Justice. In March 1954, the state security organization had, to date, its final change of name. It became the KGB, the *Komitet Gosudarstvennoe Bezopasnosti*. Since then it has had five directors. Ivan Aleksandrovich Serov held power for four years, losing the job in 1958 to Aleksandr Nikolaevich Shelepin. He ran the service until November 1961, when he was succeeded by Vladimir Yefimovich Semichastny. Under Semichastny the KGB made a number of embarrassing mistakes. Perhaps the greatest was to evolve an operation to frame as a spy Professor Frederick Baaghoorn, a political scientist from America's Yale University, who in October 1963, was visiting Moscow. The professor had served in the U.S. embassy in Moscow during World War II and with the State Department in Germany. As a result, the KGB had a file on him. That file had been summoned automatically from the vast Soviet computerized index system upon foreign nationals the day Baaghoorn had applied for his entry visa into the Soviet Union. The KGB decided Baaghoorn was ideal as a hostage exchange for a spy of theirs arrested by the FBI in New York. The Russian's cover as a chauffeur for the U.S.S.R. Amtorg trading company did not provide diplomatic immunity against an accusation of obtaining secrets from an American traitor. As Baaghoorn reached Moscow's Metropole Hotel on the night of 31 October 1963, a Russian approached and thrust documents at him. As soon as Baaghoorn instinctively touched them, he was seized by waiting KGB agents. America's President Kennedy personally involved himself when the Soviet Union offered a swap. Having been assured by every department of American intelligence that Baaghoorn was not a spy, Kennedy convened a press conference and demanded the professor's release. And obtained it.

Semichastny was replaced in April 1967, by Yuri Vladimirovich Andropov. In many ways Andropov attained the stature that Dzerzhinsky enjoyed four decades earlier; there was even a portrait of Dzerzhinsky in Andropov's apartment in Kutuzovsky Prospect. A cultured, art-loving man, fluent in English, Andropov holds the Order of Lenin, as well as having been accorded the honour of Hero of Socialist Labour. Born in June 1914, he worked as a telegraph operator before becoming a student at the Technical School of Water Transportation in Rybinsk. Soon after graduation in 1936 he became organizer for Komsomol, the communist youth movement. During World War II he fought behind the German lines. He was Soviet ambassador to Budapest in 1956 and is credited with trapping the Hungarian government leaders and thus cutting off at the head the Hungarian revolution against Soviet domination. His success in 1956 was remembered again in 1968 when the Czechs attempted a similar revolt. Andropov entered Prague immediately behind the Soviet tanks. Czech secret policemen loyal not to their own government but to the Kremlin had already prepared a list of four hundred dissidents and opposers of Kremlin rule. Those who had not already fled were arrested within five days under Andropov's guidance. Nearly all were liquidated.

As chairman of the KGB Andropov was a full member of the Politburo, in direct and daily contact with Leonid Brezhnev and the Soviet hierarchy, as every KGB chief has been since the Krushchev innovations. In May 1982, that hierarchy promoted the ambitious Andropov, a consummate politician before he became a consummate secret policeman, out of the KGB chairmanship and back into the political post of secretary to the Communist Party Central Committee. The transfer was an important one, putting Andropov in direct line to succeed the ailing Brezhnev. It distanced Andropov from a security service feared and despised within the country and viewed with disgust in the West; creating, in fact, a period to become politically and diplomatically acceptable.

That acceptability within the country took just seven months. In November 1982, Brezhnev died. And it was Andropov who made Russian political history – where Lavrenti Beria had failed – in becoming the first Soviet secret police chief to succeed to the ultimate leadership of the country.

During Andropov's chairmanship, the KGB more than at any time since Stalin, moved against questioning intellectuals and dissidents. Andropov's successor, Colonel General Vitaly Fedorchuk threatened an equally hard line, epitomized by a speech before the Supreme Soviet in the month of Brezhnev's death urging vigilance against 'imperialistic espionage and subversion'.

From 1970, Fedorchuk, a sixty-four-year-old career secret policeman, headed the KGB in his native Ukraine, one of the Soviet republics renowned for its fervent nationalism. From the moment of this appointment, Fedorchuk moved against that dissent with brutal harshness. This repression was not confined just to nationalists. Visitors suffered more harassment there than anywhere else in the U.S.S.R. and he was unrelenting in his determination to crush the growth of religion, suppressing both the Baptist and Uniate Churches.

He once wrote of the West conducting subversive activities against the Soviet Union, aiming at Russia's 'spiritual decomposition' and said its success was evident among people 'insufficiently hardened ideologically and politically, infected by nationalist prejudices and religious intoxicants or quite simply, morally corrupt'.

Fedorchuk was a dutiful disciple for such a hard line; a line which, despite the efforts of his obedient KGB at concealment by using disinformation about arms reductions and weapons disposals, Andropov continued. Burly and grey-haired, Fedorchuk entered the security service, then the NKVD, in 1939. By then the most extreme of the purges were over, but Fedorchuk had another fourteen years of Stalin's reign to learn what was expected of a Soviet secret policeman. It was a lesson he learned well. He quite properly joined the Communist Party in 1940 – as was expected – and at the time of his appointment as head of the KGB in May 1982 was a deputy in the Supreme Soviet.

Just how well Andropov prepared himself for the top political post within the Soviet Union became evident remarkably quickly.

Fedorchuk established another KGB first: that of its shortest serving head.

In November 1982, just eight months after recommending the appointment which was subsequently confirmed, the newly elevated Andropov transferred Fedorchuk to the post of Interior Minister. The move was a political one, the action of Andropov clearing out the acolytes of Brezhnev to replace them with trusted, Andropov-loyal KGB officers.

Fedorchuk's move also represented the transfer of an already proven hard-liner into a position actively to coordinate the further suppression of dissent within the Soviet Union.

Fedorchuk was not the only KGB friend whom Andropov elevated to political importance. He manoeuvred to the rank of First Deputy Prime Minister Geidar Aliyev, who until 1969 was the head of the KGB in the Soviet republic of Azerbaijan. After 1969, Aliyev was chief of the Azerbaijani Communist Party: as such he gained the reputation of a man who ruthlessly crushed provincial corruption.

Fedorchuk was replaced in November 1982 as head of the KGB by Viktor M. Chebrikov, who had been appointed in April the same year first deputy chairman of the organization. Chebrikov, like Andropov and Fedorchuk before him, is a hard-liner. Chebrikov – with a seat on the Central Committee – is a former Army general and army support had gained Andropov his ultimate post. Debts were being quickly repaid.

Chebrikov's promotion left as the KGB's first deputy the seventy-four-year-old Georgy Tsinev, who had been appointed jointly to the title with Chebrikov in March 1982 after the death of the previous – and sole – deputy Semyon Isvigun.

There was a time when Soviet leaders, including Khrushchev, denied the existence within the Soviet Union of any sort of security or espionage organization. In recent years – and particularly since Andropov's accession to power – there has been a complete change in policy. Books have been published, lauding the activities of the KGB, and speeches made praising their work. But as is frequently the case with official Soviet history, the facts are conveniently tailored to fit the appearance the leadership wishes to present. The comparisons are always made between the KGB of today and the Cheka of Dzerzhinsky's time. Ignored are the GPU and the OGPU and the

NKVD and the NKGB. If they are mentioned at all, Yagoda, Yezhov and Beria are used to illustrate the bloodthirsty megalomania of Stalin and his henchmen. Never is the point made that many of the present Soviet leadership were contemporaries of that period and had been party to the bloodshed.

Certainly, even without official prompting, the KGB look with pride upon their foundation. Today they refer to themselves as 'Chekists'. The square in front of their headquarters is named after Dzerzhinsky and his statue is its focal point.

At a New Year celebration party in 1918, Dzerzhinsky got drunk. Weeping, he wandered about in the Kremlin reception room confronting Lenin and other revolutionaries, saying again and again, 'I have spilt so much blood that I no longer have any right to live.' Like Soviet historians, the KGB is selective in what it cares to remember. Dzerzhinsky's remark is not part of its folklore. For once a Soviet security man was being too honest.

CHAPTER THREE

THE BIGGEST SPY MACHINE THE WORLD HAS EVER SEEN

In a warning handbook to diplomats and businessmen visiting the Soviet Union the British counter-intelligence directorate, MI5, described the KGB as 'the biggest spy machine for the gathering of secret information which the world has ever seen.'

In 1980 there was agreement from John McMahon, then deputy director for Operations for the CIA and now the Agency's deputy director. He said, 'The Soviets have established a worldwide network of agents, organizations and technical facilities to implement its programmes. That network is second to none in comparison to the major world powers in its size and effectiveness.'

The KGB is more.

Both the British and American opinions were describing the principal activities of the KGB *outside* the Soviet Union. Inside, the power and scope of the *Komitet Gosudarstvennoe Bezopasnosti*, the Committee for State Security, has made reality out of the Orwellian vision in its attempt to exercise Big Brother control. The KGB *is* the Soviet Union: without its omnipresent supervision of every aspect of Russian life, the totalitarian Union of Soviet Socialist Republics would cease to exist.

It is the KGB militia which guards the 41,595 miles of the country's sea and land frontiers. It monitors – through informers and emplaced officials of the respective ministries – the education in Soviet schools, academies and universities and of all the permitted arts. Through the Chief Administration for Safeguarding State Secrets in Print, GLAVLIT, it is the censor (there are 70,000 of them) for every newspaper and journal and all printed material. It directs – frequently obscenely – the sciences and medicine. It controls the police and the military. Since the demise of Lavrenti Beria, who came so close to succeeding Stalin as the Soviet dictator, the administration of prisons and labour camps has officially been split from the KGB but its power over such institutions remains. In every city, town, village and hut-cluster hamlet, the KGB has established informant networks to investigate the behaviour and attitude of the country's population of 268,800,000.

Upon attaining the age of sixteen, a Soviet citizen qualifies for an internal passport, without which it is illegal to move from one part of the country to another; it provides the KGB with a record of every official movement made by each person within Russia.

Every Soviet employee has a workbook. In it are listed his or her wage, duty, promotion, demotion, success or work failure; whether the holder is pure Russian or from one of the fourteen other Republics; or whether he is Jewish. Entries are dated. In every office, factory or collective there are KGB officers or officials. Anyone regarded as politically unreliable will be marked unsatisfactory in his workbook and fired. He must present the book to a prospective employer but no sensible employer engages someone labelled unsatisfactory. Someone without meaningful employment for more than a month in the Soviet Union is termed a parasite and there is a law against parasites: the penalty for conviction is exile or labour camp internment.

In 1977, on the sixtieth anniversary of the founding of the Russian security and intelligence service, the party leader, Leonid Brezhnev, sent the KGB a message of congratulation. He described their work as 'hard but honourable, very necessary and responsible'.

The headquarters of the KGB is, unfittingly, an ochre-coloured, ornate, wedding-cake rococo building in a square named after Feliks Edmundovich Dzerzhinsky, the founder of the organization: from his window, the present head, Viktor Chebrikov, can see the statue of the goatee-bearded Dzerzhinsky unveiled by Nikita Khrushchev in 1961. Before 1917, this seven-storey building within the long shadows of the Kremlin housed the All Russian Insurance Company. During World War II political and captured German prisoners were conscripted to build a nine-storey extension.

There was an effort to maintain the architectural style but it failed and the two buildings look as if they have been stuck together by children given different sets of building bricks for Christmas.

Behind the haphazard, uneven façade is Lubyanka prison. There are other jails, in Moscow and elsewhere in the Soviet Union, that are more modern and therefore more effective in their purpose of crushing opposition to the Soviet regime. But it is Lubyanka which retains, both inside Russia and outside in the West, the notoriety as the capital's extermination centre during Joseph Stalin's reign. It is a deserved reputation. In just four years, from 1934 to 1938, it is estimated that ten million people were slaughtered by Stalin's security directorate in the Great Purge. Among them was the cream of the revolutionary intelligentsia, the armed forces and, ironically, leaders of the intelligence service. Such people lived in Moscow and were shot in Lubyanka. The killing did not stop after 1938.

Only Chebrikov, his deputies and their immediate subordinates are allowed to enter the KGB headquarters through the original building, at the entrance to which there is now a large bas-relief of Karl Marx. Its staff has to use one of the six side entrances. Any non-KGB person wanting admission has first to obtain a permit from a separate KGB building on Kutuzovsky Prospect. The time when a visitor enters the headquarters is stamped upon his permit which is checked by guards positioned every twenty yards throughout the building. The checks are time stamped and so is the departure of the visitor: no unexplained gap is allowed in this clockworked procedure.

Dzerzhinsky Square long ago proved inadequate for the vast bureaucratic needs of the KGB. Directorate and some of the division heads retain their green-painted, carpeted or parquet-floored offices here but the main body of the headquarters staff is concentrated elsewhere. There is an enormous administrative building in Machovaya Ulitza and an even larger, ultra-modern, half-moon-shaped building off the twelve-lane Moscow ring road.

The KGB is divided into chief directorates, independent directorates and departments. Western intelligence experts

American intelligence estimates of Russian yearly expenditure on propaganda and espionage activities (1980 figures)

	$	£
Tass, the official Soviet news agency	550,000,000	296,000,000
Pravda, the official newspaper	250,000,000	134,500,000
Izvestia	200,000,000	107,500,000
New Times	200,000,000	107,500,000
Radio Moscow's foreign service	700,000,000	376,344,000
Foreign intelligence residencies attached to Soviet embassies in Western and Third-World countries	100,000,000	54,000,000
Supporting guerrilla and subversive groups in Europe, Africa, South America and Ireland	200,000,000	107,500,000
Special campaigns – such as efforts to undermine the American decision to manufacture the neutron bomb and to disrupt the installation of nuclear missiles in Europe, particularly in Britain	100,000,000	54,000,000
The campaign to hinder and prevent any expansion or improvement in what Western defence chiefs define as TNF, the nuclear force of NATO	100,000,000	54,000,000
The two different international departments of the Communist party	150,000,000	80,000,000
The press sections of the Western and Third-World embassies	50,000,000	27,000,000
Clandestine radio stations in the USSR and satellite countries transmitting propaganda to the West	100,000,000	54,000,000
Total	2,700,000,000	1,452,344,000
Total spent on propaganda	3,046,680,000	1,612,000,000
Total spent on covert action	368,550,000	195,000,000

estimate that there is a supervisory and administrative staff of 90,000. To handle the bureaucracy there are 40,000 clerks. Officials, agents and informers throughout the Soviet Union are put at 1,500,000. Abroad, the KGB is reckoned to have 250,000 operatives in the field, through embassy, legation, consulate, trade and airline personnel, suborned or traitorous nationals of the countries in which those Russians are based and 'illegals', Russian-born spies trained and equipped with entirely false identities and infiltrated into position to create espionage cells.

But these figures only refer to Russian operatives. The KGB also controls the intelligence systems of every one of its Warsaw Pact satellite countries, with some resistance from Romania. The Western-based embassies of every communist country contain spies and those spies are ultimately responsible not to Prague, Warsaw, Budapest, Sofia or Havana but to Dzerzhinsky Square in Moscow. The killer of Georgi Markov was from DS, the Bulgarian secret service; his mission had been sanctioned by the liquidation division of the KGB.

When the KGB, then called the Vecheka, was formed in December 1917, its records fitted neatly into the briefcase of Feliks Dzerzhinsky. Its budget of 10,000 roubles, equivalent to \$14,000 (£7,000) in 1982, was kept in a desk drawer by his deputy, Ia Peters.

Having had Brezhnev applaud its hard work in 1981, the KGB responded. A two-day conference in Moscow, which the party leader attended, concluded with his intelligence organization promising to 'spare no effort to accomplish the tasks of ensuring the security of the Soviet homeland.' Few security or intelligence systems have ever had an organization so elaborate to help it succeed in that task.

The construction of the KGB divides, although not perfectly, into four chief directorates, nine directorates and six independent departments, which in themselves sub-divide into subsidiary directorates, departments and service sections. Below Chebrikov each directorate is headed by its director, or *upravlyayushchii*.

The First Chief Directorate

KGB activities outside Russia are the responsibility of the First Chief Directorate, housed in the American-style building beside the peripheral route around Moscow. To accomplish its task the First Chief Directorate is sectioned into three subsidiary directorates, two special departments and eleven ordinary departments. It is here that the infiltration of specially trained Russian spies into Western and Third-World countries

The departments of the KGB

CHAIRMAN
(Chebrikov)

FIRST DEPUTY CHAIRMAN
(Tsinev)

DEPUTY CHAIRMAN

CHIEF DIRECTORATES

FIRST	SECOND	FIFTH	BORDER
Foreign	Internal	Political, Religious	GUARDS
Operations	Security	Ethnic Dissent	

DIRECTORATES

THIRD	EIGHTH	TECHNICAL	PERSONNEL
Armed Forces	Communications	SUPPORT	
	Intelligence		
		RESEARCH	SERVICES
SEVENTH	NINTH		
Surveillance	Body Guards	ADMIN	

DEPARTMENTS

SPECIAL	STATE		FINANCE
INVESTIGATIONS	COMMUNICATIONS		
COLLATION OF			
OPERATIONAL		PHYSICAL	REGISTRY
EXPERIENCE		SECURITY	AND ARCHIVES

is planned. For this purpose the world is divided into operational sections, both for detailed analysis and infiltration planning.

There are ten departments to oversee infiltration throughout the world. The First Department is responsible for Canada and the United States; the Second for Latin America; the Third for the United Kingdom, Australia, New Zealand and Scandinavia; the Fourth for the Federal Republic of Germany and Austria; the Fifth for France, Italy, Spain, The Netherlands, Belgium, Luxembourg and Ireland; the Sixth for China, Vietnam and North Korea; the Seventh for Japan, India, Indonesia and the Philippines; the Eighth for the Middle East, Yugoslavia, Turkey, Greece, Iran, Afghanistan and Albania; the Ninth for the English-speaking countries of Africa and the Tenth for the French-language countries of Africa.

The Illegals or Operations Directorate, the *destvitelni otdel*, recruits, trains and then deploys in target countries its spy-cell creating specially trained agents with false identities. The selection and training is exhaustive. Cubans, for instance, are trained for subversion and emplacement in Latin America and black Africans are taught in the Patrice Lumumba University in Moscow for eventual return and insurrection efforts against established governments in Africa, in which the Soviet Union has a particular interest because of the concentration there of strategic minerals and metals.

There are spy schools throughout the Soviet Union – some of which will later be identified – but agents intended for deep penetration into a country usually receive individual tuition at specially created and equipped apartments and houses in Moscow, Leningrad and other major cities. The precautions taken follow a basic principle of spying: an individually trained and isolated agent has no possibility of recognizing – and therefore no chance of ultimately endangering – another with whom he or she came into contact during early instruction.

Under the First Chief Directorate has been established a directorate to obtain technical and scientific secrets from the West. Its target is to monitor all nuclear, missile, microchip, space and technological progress outside the Soviet Union. It is a directorate of great size and influence within the Soviet Union, with representatives on all scientific bodies and committees and with control over the scientists of the country.

Inevitably the work of this directorate overlaps with that of the GRU – the *Glavnoe Razvedyvatelnoe Upravlenie* – the Chief Intelligence Directorate of the Soviet General Staff. The service attachés at Russian – and satellite – embassies throughout the world are responsible not to the KGB but to the GRU. They, too, are entrusted with scientific and technological espionage, particularly of war equipment. Indeed, every year a requirement list is devised by military planners and then approved by the Politburo and because of the expense involved in acquiring an aircraft or a missile, the budget allocated to the GRU is equal to that of the KGB.

The Soviet mind is a distrustful one, never satisfied with one source: the duplication, time-wasting and expensive though it may be, is regarded as justified.

The figures already charted indicate how vitally important the Soviet Union considers information. Under the aegis of the First Chief Directorate there is the information division, the *uvedomlatni otdel*, to communicate to the hierarchy the result of the Soviet Union's clandestine activities. And because the Politburo decrees that it should be presented in this manner, the intelligence is frequently channelled raw and unrefined, to the ruling body of Russia despite the existence of a separate analysis section.

But it is to disinformation that the Soviet Politburo – of which Andropov was the first full KGB member since Beria – attaches most importance.

There is no longer about the Soviet Union the romanticism of the 1930s, when intellectuals believed communism to be the salvation from the fascism of Mussolini, Franco and Hitler. Stalin has been denounced. There have been the Russian invasions of Hungary, Czechoslovakia and Afghanistan and the Russian involvement in the suppression of freedom in Poland. Today the Soviet Union is seen as a country ruled by a collective tyranny. The KGB operates under explicit Politburo instructions to counter that attitude however, whenever and wherever it can. Joseph Stalin summed up the aim when he said, 'Words have no relation to action – otherwise what kind of diplomacy is it? Words are one thing; actions another. Good words are a mask for concealment of bad deeds. Sincere diplomacy is no more possible than dry water or wooden iron.'

It is an edict never forgotten at Dzerzhinsky Square. In March 1978, the Politburo created an entirely new KGB division, the International Information Department. This new department is in addition to the existing Disinformation Department – Department A – of the First Chief Directorate. Early in 1970 Department A was upgraded to a service status to indicate its increased importance in the opinion of the Soviet leaders. Its function is to plan, co-ordinate and support Soviet propaganda operations.

One of the most secret departments within the First Chief Directorate is currently called the Executive Action Department. It is also known as Department V. Its other titles have included the Secret Division or *taini otdel*, the 13th Department, *otdel 9* or simply the code letter F.

Here assassins are trained.

Their selection is painstaking and careful; there have been defections which cause embarrassment. Particularly so was that of Nikolai Khokhlov, a captain in the death squad, who in February 1954, was dispatched from Russia to kill Georgi Sergeevich Okolovich, leader of a dissident Russian group living in Frankfurt. Khokhlov found that it was impossible to commit cold-blooded murder; instead he confessed to his victim. He later informed upon and was responsible for the capture of two other members of his assassination squad. He then gave a series of lectures on Soviet murder machinery, illustrated with cigarette-case weapons which fired poisoned bullets.

The selection of assassins does not occur until the end of the customary year-long course for an ordinary agent. The KGB attaches great importance to an agent's fitness – Moscow Dynamo, the soccer team which beat Arsenal 5–0 in Moscow in 1954, is composed entirely of KGB personnel. If, during basic training, an agent's physical prowess proves outstanding, he will be transferred for consideration by the Executive Action Department.

The killer course begins at a spy school on the corner of

Metrostroevskaya Street and Turnaninski Pereulok in Moscow. It includes rifle and pistol shooting beyond that of basic agent instruction, boxing and crippling unarmed combat. If the entrant graduates from this school, he is transferred for final instruction to a large country dacha at Kuchino, just outside Moscow. Here the training becomes specialized. There is instruction in the use of poisons and drugs which dissipate in the body minutes after being administered, giving, even under detailed pathological examination, the impression of death by natural causes. Some gases are fired from special ejector guns, subjecting the killer to the risk of the same certain death as the person he is attacking: the agents are trained to time their assaults, so that they may take an antidote pill in advance, thus making them impervious to the poison's effect. Agents are taught the use of special, battery-operated guns concealed in cigarette cases or pens. They practise vehicle sabotage, so that a fatal crash can be staged and accepted as an accident. Their unarmed combat training is perfected, so that they can isolate and deliver a fatal hit to one of the body's pressure points.

These agents are also taught organized sabotage and subversion, enabling them to operate and cause chaos to a country's communications and transport systems should an insurrection arise from which the Soviet Union considers it could benefit and with which it therefore wishes to become involved.

Monolithic though the KGB is in its overall size, it is still insufficient for the magpie-like needs of the Kremlin. Thus all the intelligence services of the Soviet satellite nations come under the direct control of the KGB and that control is exercised from within the First Chief Directorate. In the intelligence headquarters of every satellite capital sit KGB 'advisers', guiding and channelling the activities of that country's service. Throughout the Soviet Union there are training schools, isolated strictly country from country, with no fraternization and therefore with no risk of one possibly betraying another. During instruction, efforts are made to suborn agents, making them responsible not to their own countries but to Russia. The success of this manipulation was proved in 1968 when Russia moved into Czechoslovakia and two-thirds of the Czech intelligence service, the Statni Tajna Bezpecnost, declared themselves loyal not to Prague but to Moscow.

Each year the intelligence chief of every satellite country has to travel to Dzerzhinsky Square to discuss and have approved his intelligence operations for the forthcoming year. Joseph Frolik, for seventeen years a member of the Czech secret service and one of the most informative defectors ever to cross into the West, said in evidence to U.S. senators, 'Each plan specifies that the Czech intelligence service will obtain and gather political, economic, scientific, technical and military information regarding all countries which are not part of the Socialist camp, including Yugoslavia, Albania and the Chinese Peoples' Republic. Furthermore, it will conduct active measures which will exacerbate the differences between individual countries, cause tension between neutral countries and developing countries on the one hand and Western nations on the other hand.'

Still within the control of the First Chief Directorate are departments dealing with communication with overseas agents, forged passports, documents and tradecraft equipment, personnel archives and an independent personnel section. Vladimir Ilyich Lenin – who can properly be regarded as the founder of the Russian security system – said, 'We communists must use one country against another.' The First Chief Directorate exists for that purpose.

The Second Chief Directorate

The KGB's internal control of the Soviet Union is divided between the Second and Fifth Chief Directorates – there are no third or fourth.

Within the Second Chief Directorate there are twelve departments, six of which – each clearly defined by the country for which it is responsible – are entrusted with attempting to entrap and suborn foreigners in the Soviet Union and controlling their contact with Soviet citizens. The departments are broken down into sections – one attempting recruitment of foreign embassy personnel, a second to prevent the success of espionage activities by any individual embassy against Russia. There is a further section which keeps under surveillance any Russian who attempts to make contact with a foreign embassy. The Second Chief Directorate is responsible for the bugging and surveillance of all foreign diplomats, assisted by a separate technical directorate which extends its scientific electronic experimentation to poisons and clandestine murder weapons. Under the control of this Chief Directorate are sections which maintain dossiers containing information on which blackmail attempts are based: evidence of womanizing or homosexuality, for instance, for which traps can be set in specially maintained apartments, complete with microphones and camera equipment.

The First Department of the KGB's Second Chief Directorate is sectionalized to infiltrate, monitor and hopefully control U.S. embassies. And KGB chairman Chebrikov and his deputies in Dzerzhinsky Square go far beyond the American legation in Moscow's Chaikovskovo Ulitza.

It took three years to repair the roof of St Nicholas Church, opposite the American embassy in Prague. It need not have taken so long – it could have been completed within a year – but the men who swarmed the scaffolding were not interested in lining, tiling or guttering. They were KGB men whose real work involved the embassy, across the road.

The headquarters of the Czech Statni Tajna Bezpecnost is a former monastery on the Vltava river. Since 1968, KGB men have openly occupied, as advisers, administrative levels throughout the Czech service and it is these advisers who created the surveillance upon the U.S. embassy in Czechoslovakia. What happened, and is still happening, in Prague is not an isolated or extreme example. It is standard surveillance procedure upon U.S. embassies throughout the communist bloc.

In the case of Prague the only opportune difference was the positioning of the church. But KGB observation and monitoring would have been as extensive, even without the help of the position of the church. At Moscow's urging, the Czechs have altered the road system of their capital, making a series of one way and no-entry streets between the U.S. embassy and the diplomatic residential quarter, creating a regular, observed route between home and office for the American staff.

It is an illogicality between East and West that communist-bloc countries insist upon staffing their own embassies while the West employ nationals from their country of siting. Russia takes full advantage of this.

Within the Czech Ministry of Foreign Affairs is the Directorate of Services for the Diplomatic Corps. It is known by its initials, SSDS. It is staffed entirely by intelligence operatives for auxiliary local employment in embassies. Every clerk, secretary, driver, gardener, janitor, porter, translator, maid, governess and Czech-language instructor must have as a primary qualification for his or her employment a successful and good record as an agent of some section of the Statni Tajna Bezpecnost. Any repair man called into the embassy is an intelligence operative. So are the street cleaners outside the embassy and the sewer workers beneath it.

Only through SSDS can diplomats obtain accommodation. This guarantees that their apartment or house is equipped with audio-monitoring equipment in every room, including the toilet and balcony, and that the telephone is tapped. Adjoining property usually has an observation device, which is frequently a camera.

There is constant and unremitting surveillance. Observers are equipped with cars that can be disguised to prevent identification. They have rotating registration plates, their roof colour can be changed by removing a plastic foil covering, roof racks can be taken off or put on and they have either Austrian, West German or Swiss nationality tags. Some are marked 'Driving School' or 'Rescue Service'; frequently they appear to be delivery vans.

The better restaurants in Prague have tables and alcoves equipped with audio-monitoring devices and the waiters are attached to the security service. Whenever a recognizable U.S. diplomat or obviously Western businessman enters, he is shown to a table marked 'Reserved' with the explanation that the booking has just been cancelled.

A telephone call is made to the peaceful monastery overlooking the river and the restaurant identified to the duty officer by a code word. The duty officer then alerts the Sixth

Directorate of the STB, where the monitoring devices are centrally controlled and the bugged table is activated.

The extent of these KGB activities seem better fitted to the pages of spy fiction. These details are, in fact, provided by a member of the Statni Tajna Bezpecnost for almost twenty years who in 1975 gave evidence before a Senate sub-committee investigating intelligence activities of communist-bloc countries.

There is a separate department – the largest of the Second Chief Directorate – concentrating upon foreign tourists in Russia. Western experts calculate that this department – number 7 – of the KGB was allowed $525,000,000 (£250,000,000) in the six-year build up to 1980 to subvert or impress the thousands of visitors who flooded Moscow for the 22nd Olympiad. There were 10,500 interpreters and translators specially trained by the KGB. On every bus and route to and from the Lenin Stadium bordering the Moscow river there were both uniformed and plainclothed KGB operatives. Special monitoring centres were installed in the basement of newly constructed hotels at Izmailovo, next to the Izmailovskii Park metro station, the Kosmos near the Exhibition of Economic Achievements and at Dmitrovskoie Shosse. These centres listened to the electronic devices installed in every room of the hotels above. Dissidents and protestors against the Russian regime were forcibly transported from the Russian capital at the urging of this department weeks before the opening of the Olympics.

Another department has been created to observe the activities of foreign journalists in Moscow, with files upon those who are sympathetic to the regime and those who are not. Efforts to recruit foreign students on study tours to the country are regarded as sufficiently necessary and important to have a separate division and with the avalanche of material and dossiers that is created every day an entire section is allocated for maintaining the computerized records. The Eleventh Department is responsible for all travel out of Russia by Soviet citizens: usually any group of Soviet travellers is accompanied by a KGB watcher from the Eleventh Department.

The political security service – known simply by the

Russian word *sluzhba*, meaning service – marks the division of internal control over Russian people between the Second and Fifth Chief Directorates.

The *sluzhba* attempts to control daily Soviet life and it is to this service that the informant network reports. In 1969 the service was divided, four divisions remaining under the control of the Second Chief Directorate and five being transferred to the Fifth Chief Directorate. Inevitably, overlapping remains. Citizens of few countries, even at the height of wartime inventiveness, can match the Russian for black marketeering. The authorities designate it as 'economic crime' and under the Second Chief Directorate there remains a division whose aim is to crush it. There are also four divisions – corresponding with the geographical quartering of the country for KGB administrative purposes – which receive and sift the information from the informant network. Another section devoted to industrial security controls a latticework of agents and informers placed throughout Soviet industry and working life. It extends to involve itself in Russian exhibitions abroad and foreign exhibitions within the Soviet Union. It also concentrates upon foreign businessmen as possible recruits for its intelligence network.

The Fifth Chief Directorate

The Fifth Chief Directorate was created in 1969 by a Politburo suddenly confronted by the unthinkable: open dissidence. Its purpose is to crush that dissent and ensure that the restrictions imposed upon the Russian population work. To achieve that end, the KGB has resorted to the use of science and medicine that I earlier labelled as obscene.

The Serbsky Institute for Forensic Psychiatry is in Kropotkinskii Street, Moscow. Offically it is controlled by the Health Ministry. That ministry is dominated by the KGB. The Serbsky's most infamous director, Dr Daniel Luntz, who died in 1977, was a KGB colonel.

The Soviet Union is proud of the Serbsky Institute. In 1971 *Pravda*, the official Soviet newspaper, announced that the institute 'today possesses highly qualified cadres of specialists in psychiatry and the disciplines allied to it and it carries on extensive scientific research, expert pedagogical and organizational methodological work.

'It deals with such practically important problems as irresponsibility and incapacity, the prevention of socially dangerous acts, including the application of compulsory measures of a medical nature.'

In 1975 the U.S. Senate sub-committee on International Security judged the activities of the Serbsky and other KGB-dominated psychiatric hospitals in Leningrad, Kazan, Chernyakhovsk, Minsk, Dnepropetrovsk, Orel, Poltava and Kiev more objectively. Its opinion was that up to that date, seven thousand Soviet dissidents had been subjected to 'chemical lobotomy'. The standard diagnosis, of which Soviet biochemist Zhores Medvedev had been a victim, is paranoid schizophrenia. Aminazin is a drug frequently used upon political dissidents. It induces shock and depression; symptoms, in fact, that a mental patient would be expected to evidence. It creates skin sores and sometimes cancer. It destroys the memory. In the initial stages of the enforced treatment it causes a spastic-like lack of muscular control; inability to control muscular movement is an indication of mental difficulty.

Sulfazin causes a feverish rise of temperature – a typical reading is 104°F, exactly that of Georgi Markov when he was admitted to St James's Hospital – and induces acute pain from any movement of the body. It is more comfortable for the victim to remain motionless: catatonic mental patients remain motionless. Reserpine destroys the brain cells; someone with a destroyed brain is mad.

The KGB goes to extreme lengths to infiltrate and purge the dissident movements. In July 1977, a man wearing Western clothes and speaking with a strong North American accent arrived in the Georgian capital of Tbilisi. He said his name was William Fawcett and that he was a Canadian businessman. He contacted Mrs Gamsakhurdia, wife of the arrested Georgian dissident Dr Zviad Gamsakhurdia, who, with other Georgian dissidents, had set up a 'Group to Promote the Fulfilment of the Helsinki Agreement [on human rights] in Georgia'. The supposed Canadian offered to take any written material listing the aims of the group and the extent and size of its membership back to Canada. He would, he promised, set up an aid fund. Mrs Gamsakhurdia recognized it for what it was, a clumsy KGB entrapment attempt.

Georgia is not the only integrated Soviet Republic in which the KGB is attempting to control nationalistic dissent. There is unrest in Estonia and neighbouring Lithuania. In a savage attempt to crush the protest, the Soviet authorities in January 1981 put on trial its leaders, Mart Niklus, a 46-year old teacher, and Dr Juri Kukk, once a member of the Communist Party, on charges of anti-Soviet propaganda. Niklus, a political internee from 1958 to 1966 and a friend of one of Russia's foremost dissidents, Dr Andrei Sakharov, was jailed for fifteen years, with an additional sentence of internal exile. Kukk, a chemist, was sentenced to two years in a forced labour camp for defaming the Soviet system. For their trial, the smallest rooms were chosen in the Supreme Court at Tallinn; apart from Niklus's elderly parents and Kukk's wife, the only other spectators were plainclothes KGB officers.

Among the 1,500,000 Estonians, the grievances are largely political and economic; in Lithuania, the dissent is a combination of nationalism and Roman Catholicism. In 1979, forty-five Estonians – Niklus was one of them – Lithuanians and Latvians made a public demand for the three Baltic states to be independent of Russia. It was the first of several public proclamations. There followed denunciation of the Soviet invasion of Afghanistan and the staging of the Moscow Olympics.

In a letter from jail – after his pre-Olympic arrest – Niklus talked of being put into a cell 'with thieves, hooligans, pederasts, sadists and other human outcasts, who immediately wanted to rob me of everything I had.' He was later transferred to a cell in which there were thirty-two bunks for forty-eight prisoners. Niklus's bed was beneath a radiator on the floor 'in the company of many well-fed cockroaches.'

In October 1980, the anti-Soviet protests in Estonia reached the unprecedented proportions of 5,000 demonstrators marching through Tallinn, waving the banned blue, black and white flag of Estonia and chanting 'Freedom for Estonia' and 'Russians out of Estonia'. By the middle of

October, similar protests – confronted like those earlier at Tallinn by massive police suppression and arrest – had broken out at Parnu and Tartu. In Tartu workers in a machinery factory went on strike and got from a panicked Moscow investigatory commission the cancellation of raised output norms and bonus payments.

The KGB responded by demanding from mothers and fathers the identification of their protesting children on film taken by KGB cameramen. So concerned was the KGB about the unrest that Andropov himself went from Moscow personally to head an investigation. He was reported to have sacked the Estonian KGB chief, Major General August Pork. Ominously, in December, the Soviet-controlled Estonian newspapers reported the death sentences of four wartime Nazi collaborators, a familiar intimidation device.

On 9 September 1977, Leonid Brezhnev and other Soviet leaders gathered in the Bolshoi Theatre in Sverdlova Square for a glittering champagne, vodka and beluga caviar reception to commemorate the 100th anniversary of the birth of the intelligence organization's creator, Feliks Dzerzhinsky.

Surprisingly the recent erudite, cultured, art-loving multilingual leader of the KGB chose the occasion to talk about his country's dissident difficulties. Yuri Andropov said, 'Those who are misled we try to help. We try to reconvince them, to disperse their delusions.'

It was not, of course, an easy matter; one of the prime causes of dissidence was mental instability, which needed qualified hospital care. Not that Andropov liked the description of those bold enough to criticize the regime. He said, 'The very term dissident is a witty propaganda invention used to mislead the public. Using it, the Western propagandists count on presenting the situation in such a way that the Soviet system appears not to tolerate personal thoughts or persecutes anyone who steps out of line. Such a picture has nothing to do with reality.'

At the Communist Party's tenth congress in March 1921, Lenin declared, 'We have failed to convince the broad masses.' Sixty years later they are still trying.

In addition to political dissent there is the ethnic rejection of Russification by many of the Republics which have been incorporated into the Soviet Union. To oppress and destroy that disagreement, there is a department – number 6 – under the Fifth Chief Directorate. This department has survived throughout the changes that have occurred in the name and construction of the Russian intelligence and security service. It was responsible after World War II for the mass deportations of entire nations – the Kalmuks and the Crimean Tartars – from their homelands to Siberia. In 1954, a United States Congressional committee heard from a defector, Lieutenant Colonel Grigori Burlitski, how a state was destroyed because of suspected co-operation with the Nazis during the German occupation of the border regions of Russia (it was not unknown for Russians to welcome the German invaders as liberators from Stalin's rule!).

Burlitski said, 'We packed them into new lorries supplied by American aid and then into sealed cattle trucks and headed east. I would not know how many survived. The city of Novelsolskoye – the whole state of Checheno-Ingush – was a ghost area.' Burlitski said it was difficult to estimate figures: he guessed at one million people. Other estimates are lower, putting the number at fourteen thousand. There is no dispute, however, that an entire state was deported.

Under the Fifth Chief Directorate there is also a section –number 9 – with the task of controlling all printed material within the country. It is under this department that 70,000 censors work. Before publication, any book, article, play or filmscript must be submitted to censorship and approval, effectively stifling any intellectual freedom. There is, however, resistance. It creates for Number 9 its most recurrent, irritating problem. To circumvent the complete Soviet control of any free expression there has developed *samizdat*, underground photocopied, duplicated or printed news-sheets, detailing information which the state organization does not want to become public knowledge.

The best-known *samizdat* publication is the *Chronicle of Current Events*. Between 1968 and 1972 twenty-seven bi-monthly editions of this news-sheet provided truthful, accurate, detailed accounts of suppressions, summary arrests and state brutality, defying every official effort at discovery. Number 9 of the Fifth Chief Directorate of the KGB published a list of dissidents, with an ultimatum. Either the *Chronicle of Current Events* ceased publication or people on that list would be arrested and imprisoned. Publication temporarily halted. It started again in 1974, since when sixty-one issues have appeared.

There is also a division under this directorate, called *Yevsekzia*, specializing with what is referred to, with the chilling historical familiarity to Nazi terminology, as the Jewish problem. The Soviet authorities became concerned in 1972 by the increasing number of Jews wishing to emigrate to Israel. Any Jew with a job useful to the Soviet Union – in science, engineering, research – is almost automatically refused permission to leave. Intimidation is attempted against others, because the Kremlin is nervous of Western public opinion and is reluctant to have its country regarded as one from which hundreds wish to make a mass exodus. The comparatively large number that has been allowed to leave the country owes nothing to humanitarianism or to a relaxation of that concern, but rather to Western pressure imposed through trade deals vital for the Soviet Union. But even those who are allowed to leave are subjected to a wearying catalogue of pressure and extortion. Visas and permits have to be purchased. Buying a Jew's freedom has a recent, offensive precedent in the Third Reich. An arrangement – with the full knowledge and support of the Jewish division – has been made whereby western Jews and Israel move the ransom money through The Netherlands, a country whose exemplary attitude to Jewish oppression has never been properly acknowledged, to the Dutch embassy in Kalashnyi Prospect. There the would-be-emigrants collect their blood money.

For the Jews who remain the pressure is as strong as upon those allowed to leave. The three million Jews in the country represent the second largest Jewish community in the world outside the United States. For their worship, only four synagogues – in Moscow, Leningrad, Kiev and Odessa – remain in the entire country. The rest have been turned by *Yevsekzia* into clubs for Komsomol, the communist youth movement. Yeshivas, institutions of Jewish learning, have been abolished, thus no rabbis are being trained. No talis, the Jewish prayer book, are printed any more.

Shortly before his death in 1953, Joseph Stalin initiated a purge known as the Doctors' Plot, in which he alleged that a group of Jewish doctors were conspiring to murder him. There is strong belief among Jews both inside and outside Russia that Stalin intended to use the Doctors' Plot to liquidate the entire Jewish population of the country.

The Chief Border Guards Directorate

Due to the size of Russia and the responsibility involved, the militia guarding the Soviet frontiers has its own separate Chief Directorate. In the slave-minded age of eighteenth-century Britain, marines came into existence to serve upon press-gang crewed ships. Their function was to stand, face inwards, with muskets loaded whenever a man o' war was in port to prevent – and shoot if he tried – the escape of any impressed man. The Soviet border guards look inwards for defectors, rarely outwards for intruders. The border-guard militia consists of 350,000 highly trained and highly equipped soldiers. They have the latest tanks, guns, rifles, rocketry and armour; the naval division has turbo-powered patrol craft and long-range vessels equipped with every detection and monitoring device. It was this directorate that advised the East Germans on the construction of the Berlin Wall in August 1961, and improved upon the initial clumsy design by installing tank traps, man-hunting dog runs, electronic sensor areas and trip wires that trigger a Catherine-wheel burst at 100 rounds a second from concealed machine guns. The bullets are Dum Dum, soft-nosed and cross-filed. The exit wound from anyone hit effectively blows him in half.

It is this Chief Directorate, in combination with the counter-espionage division of the First Chief Directorate, that frequently stages provocateur entrapments within the borders of Russia's satellite countries fronting the nations of western Europe.

One such exercise, code-named Kamen, was carried out on the Czech side of the border in the Bavarian Forest, near the frontier with West Germany. An entirely artificial border was established, well within Czech territory, complete with 'Czech' and 'West German' border areas, tank traps, guard towers, sentries and dogs. Beyond these false border areas was built a 'U.S.' border post.

After its construction, agents of the Czech secret police, the Statni Tajna Bezpecnost, who had infiltrated dissident and émigré groups, offered to guide defectors to freedom in the West. There were five groups. Each was smuggled past 'Czech' control and then, after a conversation which the victims could witness from concealment in the woods but not overhear, they were allowed to pass on towards the American section.

The supposed American control point was perfect in every detail. Everyone wore American army uniforms. The U.S. flag fluttered from a flagpole overhead. Inside the rooms were pictures of past and present American Presidents and the U.S. army commander in Europe. The cigarettes offered were American. So were the coffee and doughnuts.

Before they could be allowed to pass further into West Germany, explained an 'American' officer, there had to be a debriefing. Each group was completely fooled, detailing past activities within the country – and often, in a disastrous attempt to impress their questioners, inventing incidents which had never occurred – and identifying dissidents and opponents of the regime remaining in the country.

After completely incriminating themselves and disclosing every detail of their remaining cells, the defectors were put into trucks, to be taken further into 'West Germany'. Within two miles, assault groups of Czech police 'intercepted' the runaways, arresting not just the defectors but, to maintain the ruse for later use, also the supposed 'Americans' who were escorting them to freedom.

In Kraslice, on the borders of East Germany and Czechoslovakia, lives and works a gardener named Hugo Mueller who has many times acted as a guide to Czechs and East Germans anxious to cross into the West. None has ever made it to freedom.

The Third Directorate

The KGB has a Services – or Third – Directorate, responsible for monitoring its armed forces. This is not to be confused with the GRU.

The KGB Services Directorate is divided into twelve departments permeating every level of military, naval and airforce life in the Soviet armed services and even beyond. It extends its strictly military function to being responsible for Aeroflot, the State airline. The Soviet Union regards Aeroflot as a support division of its armed forces, with aircraft always available to carry troops anywhere in the world; a third of the 80,000 soldiers involved in the Afghanistan invasion were carried by Aeroflot and not by military aircraft. Thus Aeroflot qualifies for the attention of the Third Directorate. Throughout the armed forces this division of the KGB has skeined a spider's web of informants.

The Politburo of the Soviet Union regards the loyalty of its armed forces as essential and vitally important. The Third Directorate ensures that loyalty.

Scientists working under the Technical Research Directorate perfected the ricin and bacteria poison that killed Georgi Markov. This directorate controls laboratories throughout the Soviet Union and its satellite countries, evolving and refining poisons which convey the impression of natural death in a victim and liquidation devices undetectable to Western forensic medicine. There is, naturally, close liaison between this directorate and the Executive Action Department of the First Chief Directorate which selects the assassins to use the weaponry devised.

Because of the vast size of the KGB separate directorates are required to govern administration and personnel. There is, further, a special directorate – number 7 – responsible for surveillance (in addition to the departments for this purpose under the Second Chief Directorate) of foreigners within the Soviet Union and Soviet citizens in contact with them.

NATO exercise planners and Western navies are used to their warships being trailed across the world's oceans by Soviet trawlers porcupined with radio antennae and bubbled with radar equipment. The responsibility for such shadowing and for intercepting foreign communication is that of the Communications Directorate. It is also known as the Eighth Directorate which can be confusing in a seven directorate organization. Inexplicably, of the seven directorates only four – the Third, Seventh, Eighth and Ninth – are numbered. The remaining three have no numbered designation, just names: Technical Operations, Administration and Personnel. The

Communications or Eighth Directorate has found its work inestimably easier with the development of space satellites and electronic eavesdropping equipment and – somewhat ironically – by the improvement of telephone communication from landline to microwave transmission, which can be easily tuned into with the properly adjusted and placed detector antennae. For years Britain's MI5 has been aware of and has warned government departments that from its aerial-roofed embassy in Kensington Palace Gardens the Russians listen to microwave telephone calls being routed through London's Post Office Tower, three miles to the east.

In 1977, the American FBI became so concerned about the success of this directorate that it warned the White House that the majority of its calls was being monitored from the Soviet embassy on Washington's 16th Street. That concern was mirrored by the Rockefeller report on the CIA. Part of its conclusion was that, 'The communist countries also appear to have developed electronic collection of intelligence to an extraordinary degree of technology and sophistication for use in the U.S. and elsewhere . . . Americans have the right to be uneasy if not seriously disturbed at the real possibility that their personal and business activities which they freely discuss over the telephone could be recorded and analysed by agents of foreign powers.'

In Washington, at least, there was some crumb of comfort. American intelligence agencies have developed in a parallel direction and at times at a superior pace to the Soviets. That same Rockefeller Commission heard evidence that the Russian eavesdroppers from 16th Street were, in fact, being bugged themselves by radio and telephone interceptors from the National Security Agency.

The extent and sophistication of Russian eavesdropping techniques became frighteningly obvious to the American authorities in 1976 when two diplomats attached to the U.S. embassy in Moscow developed lymphatic cancer and the ambassador, Walter Stoessel, unaccountably began suffering from persistent nausea and then bleeding from the eyes. Medical experts were sent from Washington and they diagnosed that the staff of the embassy, a ten-storey pre-revolutionary building in Chaikovskovo Street, was being constantly subjected to microwave radiation from electronic surveillance devices; the ambassador was particularly affected because his top-floor office was the most exposed.

The Russians did not deny beaming radiation towards the embassy. It was, they said, their method of jamming ultra-sensitive U.S. listening equipment so sophisticated that they suspected American eavesdroppers had listened in to a conversation that the party leader, Brezhnev, had conducted from his car telephone. The Americans did not deny tuning into Brezhnev's mobile conversations; they simply installed radiation shields.

The security of the Soviet hierarchy and the KGB itself is entrusted to two separate divisions. The Ninth Directorate is the bodyguard section for the Politburo and Communist Party leaders; officially officers of this department are the only people allowed to carry guns within the proximity of Russian leaders. They are responsible for their protection – and that of their families – at home and abroad.

The Department of Physical Security is responsible for the protection of the KGB. Officers attached to this section police the Dzerzhinsky Square headquarters and other buildings, ensure their security, stand twenty yards apart and time-stamp the admission passes of visitors.

There are still further ramifications of the KGB but they will be referred to and described later in this book. The chief directorates, directorates, departments and divisions that I have so far outlined are the predominant, important ones within the filigree-construction of the biggest spy machine with which the world has ever been confronted.

There are palaeontologists who argue that at a stage of its evolution the dinosaur – with its pinnacled brain and huge body mass – became so large and cumbersome it needed the buoyancy of water to allow it to move conveniently. On dry land it was clumsy: prey, even, to predators minuscule by comparison.

There are Western intelligence experts who think that the KGB has similar difficulty. The primary cause of this difficulty is the absolute refusal of Dzerzhinsky Square –

known as the Centre – to delegate any control to its operators in the field.

Every Soviet defector to the West has told the same story of restrictions and hamstringing from Moscow. In April 1954, Vladimir Petrov, Third Secretary at the Soviet Embassy in Canberra, defected. His information about Soviet spy practice caused widespread consternation throughout Western counter-espionage organizations. There was a Royal Commission investigation and part of its report said, 'Administrative control from the Moscow Centre was intensely strict and very little discretion was given to the local *rezident*. Instructions were required to be carried out to the letter in the manner directed and no deviation from the direction was permitted, save with the Centre's approval. For example the tasks for each worker were set not by him but by the Centre.'

The norm is a communist cliché and that works against the efficiency of the KGB. Norms – imposed standards of results – are demanded from every field agent and this frequently leads operatives to invent or elaborate reports rather than honestly and logically concede that there are times when there is nothing useful to pass on. In 1971, a communist-inspired insurrection in Sudan failed because the information on which it was mounted had been provided on this basis. Thus, there are occasions when, despite its organization, its technical ability, its resources and its expertise, the KGB founders like a monster in the shallows. But there are other times when it does not. In June 1918, Feliks Dzerzhinsky said, 'We stand for organized terror.' On water or on land, the dinosaur was a terrifying animal.

CHAPTER FOUR

THE GRU, THE SMALLER DINOSAUR

The *allosaurus* was one of the medium-sized dinosaurs but it was flesh-eating and ferocious. The GRU – the *Glavnoe Razvedyvatelnoe Upravlenie* – the intelligence directorate of the Soviet General Staff, is a much smaller monster than the KGB but it still kills – literally.

Surprisingly, there are conflicting opinions among Western intelligence experts whether the GRU is entirely independent of the KGB or a controlled subsidiary of the civilian intelligence organization. Those who talk of independence cite the fact that service attachés in every Soviet embassy in the West – 3,000 out of 5,200 were the figures that GRU agent-turned-informer Oleg Penkovsky quoted – are GRU operatives who work separately from KGB agents in creating cells and cultivating spies and informants. This is not evidence of independence but of the standardized procedure I have earlier described, cells distanced from cells so that discovery of one does not endanger the other.

Those who talk of control point out that the present director, General Petr Ivanovich Ivashutin, is a former deputy chairman of the KGB. But that appointment is not for the purpose of KGB control. It is the decision of the Soviet Politburo, which is determined that military chiefs will not be allowed to create the sort of exclusively private and potentially dangerous empire that Lavrenti Beria almost achieved in 1953.

The appointment of Ivashutin apart, the KGB *does* control the GRU. No one can be appointed to a position within the military intelligence organization without prior approval and clearance from the KGB. And through the KGB's military infiltration directorate that I have already outlined, it has an additional arm of control.

Penkovsky described the situation when he said: 'We do not like them and they know it. The KGB special section [for monitoring the armed forces] has its informants and co-optees among GRU officers. But we are not in a position to complain. We just have to live with them. The KGB is in the dominant position. They are the ones who investigate us and run clearances on us. It is they on whose recommendations officers are ousted from the GRU. It is they who rummage through our personal affairs, like policemen searching a suspect's hotel room. Even for a GRU officer to go abroad, KGB approval is necessary.'

The GRU has only 5,000 people spread between its headquarters in Znamensky Street, Moscow, and the operational buildings at the capital's central airport. But it is allocated a budget that matches the KGB's allowance of $368,550,000 (£195,000,000) for covert action because the GRU is responsible for obtaining all the military secrets – both defence and offensive – of the West. The GRU also trains the foreign terrorists: one of their biggest training schools is the Sanprobal Military Academy in the Crimea, another is the Higher Infantry School in Odessa. The GRU also has a training camp on Wrangel Island but no outsider is allowed there; its function is solely the training of Russians. The GRU's special Spetsnaz units are always drafted to Wrangel Island during the last few months of their final training. These men – part of a 30,000-strong specialist force – are killers, trained as assassins to be sent into the West to carry out liquidations of people whom Russia considers 'enemies of the state'. They are also organized as behind-the-lines sabotage units, to operate in the West in the event of open conflict or in any country into which the Soviet Union makes a military incursion.

The GRU trains its officers in a huge building on Moscow's Peoples' Militia Street and also in a complex twenty-five miles northwest of Moscow, centred around the village of Sezhodnya. Here the log-cabin buildings are in acres of wooded countryside, each protected by barbed-wire fencing.

Perhaps because of its smaller, more manageable size, the GRU has achieved some impressive successes. The Soviet Union's most successful spy of World War II, the eulogized Richard Sorge, was a GRU, not a KGB, man. It was Sorge's ring, operating from Tokyo, that in June 1941 warned Stalin of Germany's intention to invade Russia and who early in November 1941 discovered Japan's plan to attack Pearl

Harbor the following month. The spy cell that obtained the atomic secrets from Alan Nunn May was run by Colonel Nikolai Zabotin, a GRU officer. The theft in 1967 from the NATO base at Zell in Germany of a Sidewinder missile – it was blatantly airfreighted, like any other cargo, from Düsseldorf – was organized by the GRU. In 1977 the GRU established in France a cell which obtained operational plans of all the civil airports and their advanced electronic landing systems. In 1980 a GRU agent in Marseilles was declared *persona non grata* after being caught with plans of the latest Mirage jet fighter in his possession. The arrest led French counter-intelligence officers to the International Labour Organization in Geneva: Swiss counter-intelligence confirmed that it was a front for both KGB and GRU officers.

Apart from its headquarters numbering five thousand staff, the GRU has a staff within the Soviet Union of about 100,000. They form semi-autonomous directorates throughout each of the military districts and also within the four Soviet fleets. Within the GRU there are twenty-four sub-divisions responsible for running agents throughout foreign countries – both with and without official Russian diplomatic representation – in which the Kremlin has an interest. Within each of these twenty-four divisions there is a section to which Spetsnaz troops are attached. It was the specialized Spetsnaz troops who spearheaded the invasion of Prague in 1968 and of Afghanistan in 1979. There are indications to Western intelligence services that Spetsnaz were also present – wearing Polish uniforms – when martial law was decreed in Poland in December 1981 to crush the union liberalization there.

The GRU came into existence in 1920 and apart from the brief and already described period immediately after World War II when it passed from the control of the military to the Committee of Information it has always operated under the supervision of the military. Stalin encouraged the rivalry between the GRU and the civil security apparatus: and during the Great Purge from 1934 to 1938 destroyed much of a highly sophisticated military secret-gathering organization by liquidating its leaders.

That rivalry – in the field at least – still exists and is encouraged by the Politburo and the KGB, unthinkingly following the Western capitalist axiom that competition results in a better, cheaper and more efficient product.

CHAPTER FIVE

THE INFILTRATION OF BRITAIN

There are certain standard procedures in espionage for ensuring security. One of the most common is to run cells within cells, each separate and without knowledge of the other's existence. Aware of this, intelligence experts have a rule of thumb that for every one uncovered two more remain undetected. Following that criterion, the KGB has infiltrated Britain with disastrous efficiency.

It has implanted agents who rose to damaging levels within Britain's intelligence services. Their ability to suborn and control Members of Parliament can be gauged from evidence given in 1972 to a House of Commons appointed committee by Sir Martin Furnival Jones, then director general of MI5, the country's counter-intelligence agency, who said over one hundred MPs were known to have contact with Soviet or their satellite intelligence organizations. The Russians have established spies in the British Treasury and throughout industry. They have even – according to testimony given to U.S. senators – managed to place more than one informant close to the British Royal Family. They obtained an engine from an aircraft of the Queen's Flight: it was stripped down in the Czech embassy in London's Kensington Palace Gardens and shipped piece by piece to Moscow in the diplomatic bag.

The first Russian spy in Britain after the 1917 revolution was Maksim Litvinov, ultimately to become Foreign Minister of the Bolshevik government. Litvinov's task as Lenin's emissary was to report the international reaction to the Bolsheviks' grab for power. Litvinov found an ambivalent Britain. The Establishment was frightened. King George V had seen his relatives arrested and was trying to discover their fate, fearful at the same time that the spirit of revolution would spread to his own country. The government was nervous too, although not sufficiently so to accept Winston Churchill's demand that they formally intervene militarily.

But Litvinov detected sympathy as well, particularly in the universities of Oxford and Cambridge. In March 1919, Lenin established what was known as the Comintern, the foreign espionage arm of the Russian security service. The Comintern was to operate clandestinely throughout the world and foment what the Bolsheviks considered the inevitable spread of communism. Litvinov's feeling about the universities was remembered in 1919 and orders were given that concentrated efforts be made to recruit among the academics. Statistically Litvinov's judgment is supported by facts: more than half the declared communists or sympathizers in the 1920s attended either Oxford or Cambridge University.

But the Comintern did not restrict themselves to university recruitment: the aim there was long term, with the staggering success which was later to become obvious. There were more immediate spying needs and for that the Comintern worked through Russian trade organizations such as ARCOS.

ARCOS had offices in Moorgate Street in the City of London, under the control of the chargé d'affaires, L. B. Krassin. It was an avowed and clumsily run spy organization and it was inevitable that the British authorities would discover its existence. In May 1927 they struck. Two hundred policemen raided the offices, believing that a secret report on air strategy had been passed on to the Russians by a British spy. They failed to find it. What they did seize was three tons of documents and surprise three members of Soviet intelligence in a strongroom burning incriminating evidence. Upon one of the men police found a list of contacts and letter 'drops' used by Soviet intelligence in North and South America, Australia, New Zealand and South Africa.

The Prime Minister, Stanley Baldwin, told the House of Commons: 'Both military espionage and subversive activities throughout the British Empire and North and South America were directed and carried out from the ARCOS and Soviet delegation offices.'

It was the first – but not the last – indication of how deeply the Russians were attempting to infiltrate the country. Britain broke off relations with Stalin. Alarmed by what had happened in Britain, France and Canada swooped on Russian missions in their countries. The anti-Russian purge spread.

Among other countries which expelled Russian representatives were Hungary, Bulgaria and Czechoslovakia: what was possible in 1927 is not possible today.

This international rejection frightened the Russians. Orders were given from Moscow that espionage was to be conducted with more professionalism. It was unnecessary advice for the resident intelligence director in London, Samuel Borosovich Cahan; Cambridge and Oxford were already penetrated. Anthony Blunt, later to become art adviser to the Queen, had already been recruited as a spy and talent spotter. Harold 'Kim' Philby, son of the legendary Arabist Harry St John Philby, was an eagerly responsive choice as were Guy Burgess and Donald Maclean. Blunt lectured in French. One of his students was Leo Long, later to become an agent in MI14, wartime military intelligence, and its deputy director in Germany immediately after World War II. He also became a Soviet spy. So, too, did another Cambridge student, Michael Whitney Straight, an American who was to spy for the Russians from within the American State Department. Straight claims he provided his Soviet control, whom he names as Michael Green, with only position papers that he had authored and further claims, with rather convoluted logic, that by so doing he was actually performing a patriotic duty in providing Moscow with true assessments of American thinking. In June 1963, Straight was offered the chairmanship of an Advisory Council on the Arts, being established by President Kennedy and told that an FBI clearance would be necessary. Straight asked that his name be withdrawn from the nomination but confessed anyway to the FBI. During that confession he identified Blunt as a communist agent, an accusation he later made to Britain's MI5. Straight flew to London to confront Blunt whom, he says, told him, 'Thank God you did what you did! I was sure that it would all become known, sooner or later.' Marxist views were openly declared by M. Philips Price and W. N. Ewer. Both were students at Trinity College, Cambridge and both were to become Labour MPs. So was John Strachey, a future Labour cabinet minister who graduated from Magdalen College, Oxford.

From Oxford, too, was recruited Tom Driberg, who for

years in Parliament worked for both the KGB and Britain's MI5: a compulsive, public-lavatory preying homosexual, Driberg always carried on him an unlisted telephone number of the British secret service to arrange his discreet release after police arrest. Driberg became as promiscuous with his spying as he was with his sexual activities. He was to become chairman of the British Labour Party and elevated by Harold Wilson to the peerage as Lord Bradwell; he also spied for Czechoslovakia. From Oxford was also recruited another spy who was to become an MP, Bernard Floud.

World events gave communism intellectual appeal and by so doing aided the Comintern. By 1929 a Fascist government was already in power in Italy under Benito Mussolini. In September 1930, the Nazis became the second largest political party in Germany and Fascism was seen to be on the march. It gathered pace. In July 1936, the military commanders rebelled in Spanish Morocco, so beginning the Spanish civil war.

The Spanish civil war became an ideological as well as a military battleground. Stalin sent advisers to the Republican government of President Azaña. An international brigade – to be infiltrated, manipulated and used by the Russian security service – formed in Madrid to oppose General Franco and the third manifestation of Fascism to threaten Europe. To be a communist was fashionable; responsible, too. It meant you were a fighter for freedom. Kim Philby reported on the war for *The Times* in London and on Franco's forces for the Comintern to Moscow. There were occasions when Guy Burgess acted as his courier.

World War II provided the Russians with their greatest opportunity to expand their intelligence organization. After Hitler broke his peace pact with Stalin in June 1941, the Russians became allies of the West and at once Moscow made demands for shared intelligence secrets. They were already receiving some which, had he known about it, would have driven Churchill into a rage. Since the 1920s Churchill had never lost his distrust of Russia and the communists and was reluctant to share with them any more intelligence than was absolutely necessary. He was particularly anxious that Stalin should not learn of Britain's ability to read Enigma.

Enigma was the code by which the German naval and air force high commands conducted their secret communications. It was, too, the code which Hitler used for his liaison. The British ability to read it was one of the major intelligence breakthroughs of the war.

The system worked by having what amounted to two electric typewriters side by side and linked by a complex electrical wiring system, the Enigma. Using a pre-selected book of keys, identifying the time of day, the day of the month and the month of the quarter, the message was written on the left-hand machine and enciphered, through electrical connection, on to the right-hand machine, from which it was transmitted. When it arrived at its destination, an operator set the keys of a similar apparatus in the way instructed in the message, typed the signal out on the left-hand machine, passing it through the Enigma translator and receiving a plain-language message on the machine to his right. The daily change of key guaranteed that the code was unbreakable. So complacent were the Germans that their code was inviolate that they provided Japan with it and installed it in their ships and submarines, satisfied that it would remain meaningless if it were captured. Hitler was unaware that even before the outbreak of the war Britain had obtained, through co-operation with France and Poland, a copy of the Enigma machine. And that a Polish Jew expelled because of his race from Germany, where he had worked in the Enigma manufacturing factory, had made a replica of the German device for British intelligence.

From the information available, British cryptanalysts had manufactured a keyhole-shaped machine, eight feet tall and eight feet wide at its base, which could transcribe the intercepted messages without the need for the daily key.

Enigma was accorded the highest security classification. The code name of the deciphering machine, nicknamed The Bomb, was Ultra. Hitler never knew Britain had this machine; Stalin learned about it within months of entering the war on the side of the West.

- Ultra was housed in Hut 3 in the parklands of the Government Code and Cypher School at Bletchley Park, in Buckinghamshire. To Bletchley Park in 1942 was posted a

fluent German speaker who had been talent-spotted at
Cambridge by the homosexual Anthony Blunt. His name was
John Cairncross. From 1936 he had worked in the German
department of the Foreign Office. But Maclean was already
established there as a Russian spy. Upon Moscow's instructions, Cairncross transferred to the Treasury. For four years
he provided Dzerzhinsky Square with all the details of
Britain's war economy. In 1942 he used his fluency in
German to gain a transfer to Bletchley Park. And from there
on a weekly basis he passed Ultra secrets to his Soviet contact in
London, Anatoli Gorsky. From Cairncross the Russians
learned the German air dispositions before the Battle of
Kursk. After the war Cairncross returned to the Treasury and
remained an active agent until 1952 when he retired to live in
Italy.

The Russians had other important spies in place. By now
Philby, with the help of family connections, had left journal-
ism to join Britain's Secret Intelligence Service. For Moscow,
this was a coup: quite rightly they concluded that someone of
Philby's ability could entrench himself sufficiently firmly to
remain and rise in the country's intelligence service in the
post-war period. Philby infiltrated well, crossing the barriers
between MI6 and MI5 and carefully exacerbating the feuds
that existed among his immediate department chiefs. Upon
his own admission, Philby utilized his position to examine
every available archival record concerning the Soviet Union.
Everything went back to Moscow. He also provided biographical records on every intelligence officer he encountered.
He continued to do both after the war. By the summer of
1943, Philby was in charge of Italian counter-espionage, as
well as being responsible for that in Africa, France and the
Iberian peninsula. He was later to rise higher.

Guy Burgess had been involved with intelligence for the
previous three years, entering in the haphazard way of
wartime recruitment through the BBC to a section supposedly
devoted to broadcasting propaganda and the planning of
sabotage behind enemy lines. Like Philby, Burgess did not
confine himself to his department but became a magpie
collector of information throughout MI5. Because of his
drinking and homosexual philandering Burgess's value to the

Russians is sometimes underestimated. It should not be. His worth to Moscow is well summed up in evidence given by Vladimir Petrov, the KGB agent who defected in Australia in April 1954. In evidence to an Australian Royal Commission the following year, Petrov recalled a conversation with Filip Kislytsin who was for a time Burgess's Soviet controller in London. According to Petrov, Kislytsin told him, 'The volume of material Burgess supplied was so colossal that the cipher clerks of the Soviet Embassy were at times almost fully employed in enciphering it so that it could be radioed to Moscow, while other urgent messages had to be dispatched in diplomatic bags by couriers.'

Anthony Blunt had also insinuated himself into MI5 and was Burgess's nightly accomplice in collating and photographing material. So great was its volume that when the Russians provided them with a camera to take their own photographs – rather than have the material delivered to the Soviet embassy for copying – the two complained that the extra work meant they could not get sufficient sleep.

Burgess's value went beyond what information he could collect from his daytime activities. Like Tom Driberg – for a time the William Hickey gossip columnist on the *Daily Express* – Burgess's value lay in the titbits of gossip and possible blackmail-pressure scandal that he could obtain. At the time he occupied a flat at 5 Bentinck Street, London, let to him by a Cambridge undergraduate friend, Victor Rothschild, of the banking family. To this flat were invited nightly an assortment of homosexuals, politicians and intellectuals from whose conversation Burgess – frequently not as drunk as he appeared – collected more information for the overworked encoders at the Soviet embassy. Otto Katz, with the cover of a Czech diplomat but in reality a long-serving member of the Soviet Comintern, frequently attended.

In November 1943 in Teheran, Churchill, Roosevelt and Stalin tried to draw up a map of Europe as it would appear after the war. A depressed Churchill found both the other world leaders opposed to him. Churchill records that Stalin talked of the necessary mass execution of 50,000 leading Germans and put at four million the number of German slave labourers he would need to rebuild a war-ravaged Russia.

'Whether he was joking or not could not be ascertained,' wrote Churchill. Stalin was not joking. Before Yalta Churchill had written, in April 1944, 'We are purging all our secret establishments of communists because we know they owe no allegiance to us or to our cause and will always betray secrets to the Soviet, even while we are working together.'

By 1944 it was too late.

By then Burgess had moved from his loosely defined but valuable post to join the Foreign Office press department. And Philby was intriguing for a position that even his Russian controllers could not have imagined when he joined British intelligence – head of Section 9, which was shortly to be created in order to investigate and infiltrate the Soviet espionage organization. At the end of 1944 he got the job.

The ending of the war – like its beginning – was favourable to Russia. Less than a month before, on 12 April 1945, Roosevelt died. His untried and inexperienced Vice-President, Harry Truman, succeeded to the office and to the conference table at Potsdam. The conference was fixed for July. The National Government in Britain, headed by Churchill, ended on 23 May; the wartime leader went to Potsdam as a caretaker premier, leaving a general election in London which was to take place on 5 July. Clement Attlee was an adviser to Churchill but the conference ended with Attlee being elected Britain's leader, after the shock defeat of the Conservatives by Labour. Now only Stalin had the stature of a statesman who had controlled his country throughout the conflict. And he remained obdurate against every demand that Russia should quit the countries of Eastern Europe they had over-run in pushing back Germany.

In London Attlee chose Ernest Bevin as his Foreign Secretary. Bevin asked Hector McNeil to be his Minister for State. McNeil, a frequent guest at Bentinck Street, invited Guy Burgess to be his personal assistant. Into the Cabinet, as Minister for Food, went John Strachey, the former Cambridge colleague and now declared ex-communist but still a visitor to Bentinck Street. Nine other MPs who at one time had embraced the communist doctrine entered the House of Commons under Attlee's leadership, as well as two openly declared communist candidates.

Three and a half thousand miles away in Washingto[n]
Donald Maclean was in place as First Secretary in the Briti[sh]
Embassy, a vital link with the country which had explode[d]
two atomic bombs, the secrets of which were being leaked [to]
Moscow from Ottawa by a former Cambridge friend [of]
Maclean's, Dr Alan Nunn May. Maclean was a diligen[t]
conscientious worker. Soon he was deputizing for Mich[ael]
Wright, the Head of Chancery. It gave him access to ev[ery]
communication of importance moving through the embass[y.]

In the spring of 1946 the new British ambassador, [Sir]
Archibald Clark Kerr, later to become Lord Inverchap[el,]
arrived in Washington. Sir Archibald took with him the g[ift]
he brought from his previous posting, Moscow. The pres[ent]
was his Russian valet, a personal gift from Stalin. The va[let]
(dressed like a Cossack) appeared to think – because he w[as]
never told otherwise – that the most classified areas of [the]
embassy were open to him. It was with great reluctance t[hat]
Sir Archibald acceded to discreet pressure from American[s as]
well as from British security and had his diminutive a[nd]
almost constant companion returned to Moscow, through [the]
Russian embassy in the American capital. British intellige[nce]
believed that the Soviet security service was as disappoin[ted]
as the ambassador.

In 1947, having formed his Russian desk, Philby w[as]
transferred to active intelligence gathering in the Brit[ish]
embassy in Turkey. Guy Burgess made an ostensible holi[day]
visit, maintaining contact. In Turkey Philby heard, too, t[hat]
British intelligence had engaged someone Philby had tale[nt]
spotted. The man's name was George Blake. It was not u[ntil]
Blake was sentenced to forty-two years in prison in 1961 t[hat]
Philby learned that, like himself, Blake was a double ag[ent]
who had exposed to the Russians from its inception [the]
$30,580,000 (£11,000,000) construction by English [and]
American intelligence officers of a tunnel from West Be[rlin]
into East Berlin to tap Red Army telephone communicatio[ns.]
Alerted to its existence, the Russians had for years fed M[I6]
and the CIA with false information.

While Philby and Burgess were enjoying the sunshin[e of]
Istanbul, American intelligence discovered the activitie[s]

Maclean. It occurred in an appropriately labyrinthine way. During World War II, a close relationship had been formed between the London-based Jewish intelligence organization and James Jesus Angleton, who served in Britain with the forerunner of the CIA, the Office of Strategic Services: Angleton was later to become a brilliant counter-espionage chief for the Agency.

Two years earlier, in 1945, Maclean had been appointed joint secretary of the Western Allies' combined policy committee on atomic development. It provided – in addition to the information already being passed on by Nunn May and Klaus Fuchs – a priceless source of material for the Soviets. But expert guidance was needed for the unscientific Maclean. It was provided by another Englishman, a homosexual physicist codenamed Basil who was co-ordinator of several nuclear development committees and an active Russian agent. It was Basil's identity that the Jewish intelligence disclosed to Angleton. The CIA man – whose creed was 'The spy you know is always better than the one you don't' – offered him immunity in exchange for co-operation. Basil agreed and named Maclean as a spy.

Angleton's allegiance was to America, not to Britain. He did not pass the information on to London. Independent evidence had also arisen of a spy within the British embassy. American cryptanalysts monitoring radio traffic from the Russian mission in New York had broken a code and traced the embassy as the source of the material being carried on it. Angleton decided to let the British learn that they had a KGB spy through the codebreakers, who were co-operating with London.

In 1948, Maclean was transferred from Washington to Cairo. A year later, having betrayed to the Russians all the secrets passing through the British embassy in Istanbul, Philby was moved to Washington as British intelligence liaison officer with the FBI and the CIA. From Basil the spy-catcher, Angleton, learned that Philby was a Russian agent. Again, he did not tell the British about the spy he knew might lead him to others.

In Moscow Lavrenti Beria, the cosmopolitan spymaster, was beginning to realise the benefits of the satellite countries that the Soviets had refused to give up. There was resistance and rejection from many of the occupied countries' intelligence services but his infiltration was patient. Gradually they began to work for Russian intelligence: diplomats and spies from the satellite countries began arriving in London to cultivate cells of their own, for Moscow's benefit.

Both Philby and Burgess knew that the American code-breakers had intercepted material provided by Maclean. And Burgess, a former lover of Maclean's, warned him. In 1950, Burgess was posted to Washington, as Second Secretary. By now Burgess had moved from Bentinck Street to another apartment in Lower Bond Street. He gave a farewell party there. Hector McNeil, promoted into the Cabinet as Secretary of State for Scotland, attended. So did McNeil's successor at the Foreign Office, Kenneth Younger. Anthony Blunt was also a guest.

In Washington, Burgess moved in with Philby. Burgess had always been an outrageous dissolute: he had been posted to Washington with the warning that it was his last chance to reform. He did the opposite, scandalizing the diplomats with whom he had to work. Basil told Angleton there was another Soviet spy in place.

In Cairo the strain proved too much for Maclean and he had a nervous breakdown. After psychiatric treatment, he returned to the Foreign Office in Whitehall where he was offered the American department. By 1951 the cryptanalysts and investigators of the Russian radio traffic had narrowed down the list of suspects from the Washington embassy. Maclean's name was on it. Philby saw the list and twice he motored out of Washington, for informative meetings with his Soviet controllers. He suggested that Burgess should be the man to tell Maclean that the net was finally about to close in on him. The Russians agreed and Burgess was briefed. Burgess succeeded in being sent home in an almost farcical fashion, driving his 12-cylinder Lincoln so fast through Virginia that he received three speeding tickets which he refused to pay, pleading diplomatic immunity.

Maclean had already been positively identified as the source of the Washington embassy leaks when Burgess arrived in London in May 1951; he was under what intelligence officers of the time called 'loose surveillance'. High-grade material was being withheld from him. The two men met several times that month, in Maclean's Foreign Office chambers. Burgess told Maclean an escape plan was being prepared.

Maclean's interrogation was fixed for 28 May. A week before, Philby used Burgess's abandoned Lincoln as an excuse for a warning cable. It appeared to be nothing more than a reproach for carelessness in failing to dispose of the vehicle properly before his return to England. Unless Burgess acted at once, said Philby, 'I would send his car to the scrap heap.' Burgess got the real message.

Maclean's loose surveillance by the British security service ended, inexplicably, at the ticket barrier of Charing Cross station, where he caught the train to his home in Tatsfield. Burgess drove in a hired car from London to Tatsfield. They had dinner with Maclean's heavily pregnant wife, Melinda. And then they left, to drive to Southampton to board the cross-channel ferry to St Malo and eventual sanctuary in Moscow.

From Washington, the CIA director, General Walter Bedell Smith, informed London that Philby was no longer acceptable as the SIS liaison man. Philby flew home to interrogation at the hands of MI5 director, Dick White. It was the first of eleven separate interviews over the next two years with a variety of intelligence officers all concerned at the collapse of the British–American intelligence relationship caused by the affair. At each interrogation there was suspicion, but no proof. As one of the interrogators told me: 'Philby had been in from the beginning; he knew as much as we did. I knew he was guilty but I couldn't prove it. And we're not the KGB.'

Others were not so fortunate in being dealt with on suspicion alone. Ten officials of the Foreign Office were forced to leave because their loyalty could not be established positively. Twenty-three more were cautioned. John Cairncross was unmasked. Sir Norman Brook, Secretary of the Cabinet, chaired a working party which introduced a system of 'positive vetting' for existing civil servants and for future new entrants. It was an improvement upon previous recruitment procedure but it was not foolproof.

The Burgess and Maclean affair became stale news. Philby was put out to pasture, avoided by his Soviet controllers and all but a few of his most trusting intelligence friends. In 1953 Stalin died; in London, Philby had no idea of the convolutions taking place within the intelligence organization in Moscow for whom he had so long been a diligent worker.

A year later Vladimir Petrov, a disciple of the purged and executed Beria, chose defection rather than return to Moscow and a possible executioner's bullet in the underground cells of Lubyanka. From his friendship with Filip Kislytsin, their London controller, Petrov knew – and disclosed – that Burgess and Maclean had been recruited during their undergraduate days at Cambridge. And that a 'third man' had warned them of impending arrest and led to their escape to Moscow. The information was still unpublished and Dick White asked Anthony Eden, then Foreign Secretary but who was more interested in taking over the premiership from the ailing Winston Churchill, for permission to publish and unsettle the still secure Philby. Eden, intent upon the occupancy of 10 Downing Street and unwilling to resurrect old scandals, refused. In September 1955, the *People* newspaper disclosed in an interview with Petrov the existence of the third man. Over the next months there followed an almost unbelievable sequence of political blunders, opportunism and mistakes. The MP for Brixton, Marcus Lipton, privately prompted by an exasperated but hopeful British secret service, named Philby within the legally protected chamber of the House of Commons. On 7 November the Foreign Secretary, Harold Macmillan, publicly cleared Philby in a Parliamentary statement. The following day a confident Philby stage-managed a press conference at his mother's flat, refuted every allegation and demanded that Marcus Lipton repeat the allegation outside the House of Commons, so that he could be sued for libel. Like the security officials, Lipton had only suspicion but no proof. He withdrew the accusation in a Commons apology. Russia's spy was still safe.

For a security organization that had been overhauled and in which a system of positive vetting had been established, what happened in the following years is as astonishing as withdrawing the surveillance from Donald Maclean once he was comfortably installed in the corner seat of his commuter train from Charing Cross. Philby's long-time friend, Dick Brooman White, a former intelligence colleague who had become an MP, pressurized the Foreign Office to find re-employment for Philby. He enlisted the support of MI6 Director, Sir John Sinclair. Their joint approach persuaded *The Observer* and *The Economist* to use Philby, the Soviet spy journalist of the Spanish civil war, as a correspondent in Beirut.

Philby snatched at the opportunity. So did his KGB controllers, given the chance to re-activate him in a volatile and increasingly important part of the world. And so – most astonishing of all – did British intelligence. It was not until December 1961 that Philby was denounced categorically as a Soviet spy. The information came from Anatoli Golitsin, a major in the First Chief Directorate of the KGB who defected in Helsinki. But this information did not go to the British but to the Americans: James Angleton was anxious to debrief Golitsin about a possible Russian spy within American intelligence and did not make Golitsin available to the British until 1963. By then, Philby had had eighteen months' warning of his exposure. Aware of the information Golitsin could provide, the KGB made Anthony Blunt pay a warning visit to Beirut. Showing both the ineffectiveness of British counter-intelligence and the amazing arrogance of the Soviet spies, Blunt travelled to the Lebanon with his lover, John Gaskell, and actually stayed in the official residence of the British ambassador to the Lebanon, Sir Ponsonby Moore Crosthwaite.

The final confrontation with Philby had about it the amateurishness of all his previous encounters with a suspicious British service. British intelligence has no power of arrest: that has to be performed for them by Scotland Yard Special Branch. And Lebanon is outside British legal jurisdiction. So Nicholas Elliott, a former colleague, friend and British intelligence resident in Beirut, was sent back directly to accuse Philby with the accumulated, unarguable evidence of twelve years of investigation. Philby confessed. He admitted everything but withheld the identity of any of his Soviet contacts. Elliott went back to London for consultation with MI6 director, Sir Dick White. Elliott urged Philby to follow to clear the matter up finally. Still blinkered by old school morality and mentality, Elliott said it would be the right and proper thing to do.

Two years before, George Blake had returned, not after such a confrontation but on the promise of discussing a promotion. And he was not an old public schoolboy. He was sentenced to forty-two years imprisonment at the Old Bailey. Philby had one more meeting in Beirut with Blunt. On 23 January 1963 he vanished. He reappeared in Moscow.

In London other spy systems were already established. From an £18-a-week flat on the top floor of Pelham Court, Fulham Road – the telephone number was 8955 – in the expensive London district of Kensington, a KGB resident named Nikolai Korovin ran cells of unbelievable value to Moscow.

Korovin controlled the Portland spy ring, in which two employees of the Naval Underwater Research Establishment at Portland, Dorset – Harry Houghton and his mistress, Ethel Gee – supplied the top secrets of Britain's submarine and underwater research and development to a man they knew as Gordon Lonsdale. He was, in fact, a Russian 'illegal' whose real name was Konon Molody. In Vinnitsa, in the Ukraine, the KGB has created an entire Western city, complete with Western shops, transportation, accommodation, telephone boxes and systems. It even has a Western name: Clifton. Part of it is composed of a Canadian section and here Molody was stripped of his real identity and took on instead that of Gordon Lonsdale: before entering Britain, he was based in Canada. Having arrived in London, he became the link between Korovin and the Portland cell, which also included radio operators, Peter and Helen Kroger, from whose bungalow in Ruislip, Middlesex, the information was transmitted to Moscow.

The Portland spy ring was the classic example of the cell within a cell construction of an intelligence operation that I described at the beginning of this chapter. Molody was a trained, hardened professional, confident that he would be exchanged rather than serve the imprisonment imposed upon him and he did not disclose the identity of 'Roman', Korovin's codename.

Had he done so, then British intelligence might have discovered earlier the existence within the Admiralty of William Vassall, who was also run by the KGB man. Vassall, a practising homosexual, had been employed in the naval attaché's office at the British embassy in Moscow in 1955. His sexual inclinations were quickly realized by the Russians. He was compromised and blackmailed and from that time – in exchange for money with which he lived far beyond his means but to the apparent ignorance of British security – he passed over secrets to the Russians. In Moscow he was useful. Upon his reassignment in London, he became invaluable. He was appointed a clerk to the headquarters of naval intelligence, with unrivalled access to secrets.

Korovin ran Vassall and transmitted to Dzerzhinsky Square hundreds of those secrets. They did not stop with Korovin's return to Moscow in 1961. Before his departure Korovin handed over control of the Navy clerk to another KGB man, Nikolai Karpekov.

But neither the Portland spy ring nor Vassall was Korovin's greatest source of information. That was George Blake. Until his posting to Beirut in 1960, to undergo a course in Arabic, Blake – who during his Berlin posting had shown his loyalty to Moscow by disclosing the secrets of the Allies' listening tunnel and warning the Russians of an impending defection of a GRU colonel who was seized and liquidated – sat for long hours at Pelham Court, identifying everyone in British intelligence with whom he came into contact during his training and subsequent service.

By now the seeds that the disgraced and executed Beria had planted in the intelligence organizations of Russia's dependent countries began to bear fruit. Harry Houghton had originally been recruited by the Poles when he was attached to the British embassy in Warsaw, to be taken over by the KGB when they realized the value of his posting to Portland.

The Czechs proved particularly useful to the Russian service. After World War II British intelligence created a special section (C-10) staffed by Czech officers and operatives who had left their country rather than live under impending communist rule. There was a control desk in London and over one hundred agents were in place throughout the Middle East, Scandinavia, Austria, Switzerland, Belgium and The Netherlands.

In London a staff officer of the Czech section, disaffected

because he considered himself wrongly passed over for promotion, approached the Czech embassy. He was recruited and accorded the code name 'Light'. Over a two-year period he disclosed the identities of the hundred agents, together with those of their British controllers and liaison officers. More than a third were liquidated by the Statni Tajna Bezpecnost and the KGB before British intelligence reacted, disbanding the service. From the agent, 'Light', the Czechs knew the office which housed the section created in their name. They watched it, seeing the files being loaded into removal vans. By following the vans, they located the headquarters of MI6, then Leconfield House in Mayfair's Curzon Street.

Instructions were sent from Moscow through Prague to the Czech embassy in Kensington to cultivate particularly British MPs. One of these who became an agent was Will Owen, Labour member for Morpeth.

Frantisek August, for fifteen years a member of the Czech service, explained the reasoning behind the Moscow demands when he gave evidence before a U.S. senate committee in Washington in 1976. He claimed that the Soviet Union quite expected the West militarily to oppose the creation of the Berlin Wall and prepared battle contingency against it.

August said, 'In my British section, KGB advisers instructed us to prepare a list of British intelligence and counter-intelligence facilities that would have to be secured immediately in the case of an invasion of England. Lists were prepared also of persons hostile to the Soviet Union, including MPs and journalists. These were to be arrested immediately upon the occupation of England. Similar measures were prepared for all countries of Western Europe.'

August fled from Czechoslovakia after the Russian invasion of his country in 1968. So, too, did Joseph Frolik. In evidence to a sub-committee of U.S. senators in 1975 Frolik gave further proof of KGB-initiated infiltration in Britain.

After Harold Wilson became Labour Prime Minister in Britain in 1964 he ordered that no MP could be investigated by MI5 without his specific permission. That permission was sought as a result of what Frolik told his American questioners. Frolik named Captain Robert Husak – a known and

senior Czech intelligence officer in London – and Josef
Kalina, alias Karhan, as contacts of a leading member of
Wilson's government, John Stonehouse.

Stonehouse who later staged a disappearance by drowning
from Miami Beach, only to be discovered in Australia in
December 1974, returned to Britain and be sentenced to
imprisonment for fraud, theft and deception, held a number
of posts in the Wilson administration. From 1964 to 1966 he
had been Parliamentary Secretary to the Ministry of Aviation.
For a year after that he was Under Secretary of State for the
Colonies and then Minister for Aviation. From 1967 to 1968 he
was Minister of State for Technology and the following year
Postmaster General. He was then Minister of Post and Tele-
communications from 1969 until 1970.

Stonehouse's interview by security officers was conducted
in the presence of Harold Wilson. Stonehouse admitted
knowing the named officers, whom he had met during his
ministerial duties, but firmly denied ever being recruited as
an agent. The denial, subsequently repeated, was accepted by
Wilson.

The allegation against John Stonehouse was not the only
one made by Frolik. He said the KGB had become convinced
that, because he was unmarried, the then Conservative party
leader, Edward Heath, had homosexual tendencies and could
be compromised. Aware of Heath's love of music, they
managed to involve a Czech homosexual organ virtuoso in a
recital that the British premier was to conduct. The planned
entrapment failed because their suspicions about the one-time
Tory leader were quite unfounded. Frolik identified the KGB
agent as Jiri Reinberger, who died in Prague in May 1977.
Named Artist of Merit in 1964, Reinberger was the composer
of three organ concertos, two symphonies and a cello
concerto.

The recital was not the only occasion, according to Frolik,
when the KGB used the arts in their intelligence efforts. He
alleged in his evidence to the Senate sub-committee that
during Princess Margaret's marriage to Lord Snowdon the
Czechs succeeded – on the orders of Moscow – in getting an
agent close to the Royal couple through Lord Snowdon's
interest in the theatre. Frolik identified the informant as a

director who has had a renowned and distinguished career in
the Czechoslovakian theatre and who met Lord Snowdon
during a photographic assignment for the *Sunday Times* in
1965. The man is a member of the communist party, the
self-educated son of a peasant farmer. Frolik said that as a
deception manoeuvre to gain the man friends in the West, he
was reported to be under pressure from Moscow-imposed
hardliners after the collapse of Dubček's liberalization in
1968. As part of that cover, he was dismissed as director of a
leading Prague theatre and denied permission to visit Britain,
a decision which led famous British theatrical names such as
Sir Laurence Olivier, Paul Scofield, Trevor Nunn and Dame
Peggy Ashcroft to sign a protest.

Frolik also named as KGB agents a famous Czech Olympic
athlete – so cynical, claimed Frolik, that the man even
informed upon his wife while all the time enjoying a
reputation in the West as an anti-communist – an equally
famous Soviet poet allowed easy access to the West to
infiltrate and report upon the artistic developments in
America and Europe and leading Czech figures in ice-figure
skating, international bicycling and ice hockey.

The most unusual claim came from Frantisek August. He
said in evidence in Washington that in 1962 orders of the
highest priority came from Moscow to obtain an engine of an
aircraft of the Queen's Flight for KGB examination. Cautious
of direct involvement in case there was an embarrassing
discovery, the KGB entrusted the Czechs with the job. The
Statni Tajna Bezpecnost decided that to attempt to steal the
engine would be too dangerous, convinced the security would
be absolute. For just such purposes, the Czechs have an
intelligence-backed but legitimate trading company, called
Omnipol. It made trade enquiries and learned that periodi-
cally, as part of routine servicing, engines were replaced and
that the old equipment was sold as normal surplus. August
said Omnipol paid £30,000 for an engine which was dis-
mantled at the Kensington Palace Gardens embassy, shipped
in the diplomatic bag to Prague and from there immediately
sent on to Moscow. Although it was a Russian request, he
added that the Czech Ministry of Foreign Affairs had to settle
the bill.

An agent whom August ran in London during the early 1960s was someone given the codename Marconi. His real name was Nicholas Prager. At the time he was serving as a sergeant in the Royal Air Force and supplied the Czechs with drawings, blueprints and photographs of the Blue Diver radar jamming device. The material was sent direct to Moscow. August insists that a letter of thanks came from the office of the Soviet premier, actually signed by Nikita Khrushchev, who in 1953 had defeated Beria's attempted coup and concentrated ultimate control of Russia's intelligence organization under the direct control of its political leaders.

Prager left the Air Force and started work with English Electric, in their computer section. He still supplied his Czech and Russian controllers with classified information about computer development, on one occasion advising them to delay the purchase of two intended American machines until improved models, of which the Czechs and Russians were unaware, became available.

Later, in 1971, Prager was jailed for twelve years for his espionage activities. He was released after only six years. He was Viennese born and the sentence had meant that his 1948 naturalization was taken from him: because they were unsatisfied about his nationality Czechoslovakia – the country he had served so dutifully – would not grant him permission to settle there. He was allowed to remain in Britain, where he died in 1981.

Joromir Johanes was in London in the early 1960s under cover of press attaché. Although a Czech, he worked directly for the KGB. His function was recruitment – in Russian *verbovochnaya baza* – particularly of MPs. I have earlier referred to the Oxford recruitment of Bernard Floud, son of Sir Francis Floud and Labour MP for Acton, who committed suicide in 1967 after questioning about his KGB contacts; and to Will Owen, Labour MP for Morpeth who in 1970, aged sixty-eight, was to appear in court on charges brought under the Official Secrets Act. Owen, who admitted receiving £2,300 ($5,520) from the Czechs, was acquitted on the grounds that the information he provided was not classified.

The primary purpose of recruiting MPs is not for the information they will provide, although this is obviously important if they reach some key position. Their most useful role however is seen as 'agents of influence'. I have already made the point that the Soviet Union considers $3,046,680,000 (£1,612,000,000) a cheap-enough price for influencing Western opinion. According to the Director of MI5, by 1970 over one hundred members of the British House of Commons had questionable relations with Russian or East European contacts.

Ladislav Bittman is a former deputy chief of the disinformation department of the Czech service, having previously served for eight years directing and recruiting agents. His information contributed to Sir Martin Furnival Jones's later assessment of the extent of Parliamentary infiltration. Bittman said, 'They [the MPs] received instructions to initiate and influence Parliamentary discussion on public issues the Soviets considered important for their official diplomatic manoeuvring against Britain . . . I cannot tell you the names because I don't know them, but our department conducted several operations in which members of Parliament were used for making certain statements initiating certain discussions and creating a situation or atmosphere that official Soviet policy could use or misuse for manoeuvring. I cannot tell you either the names or the specific issues. I don't remember the issues any more and I don't want to create any witch-hunts for Britain. But I say this is a fact – the Czech service had at the time several agents among members of the British Parliament.'

One, as I have already said, was Will Owen. His use was extended beyond this purpose, because he was a member of the Parliamentary Estimates Committee. Upon this committee sit MPs – the membership has fluctuated from forty-three down to thirty-three with the establishment of specialist sub-committees – who consider every detail and aspect of British parliamentary expenditure. During Owen's membership, the committee considered Royal Navy, Army and Royal Air Force spending, also that of government departments, spanning everything from Foreign and Commonwealth, communication, trade, industry, agriculture, local industry, social services, science and education. Eventually these figures are debated publicly in the House of Commons. Thus, technically, the defence put forward at Owen's trial that the information he provided was not secret was justified. What did not seem to be appreciated was that House of Commons discussion is wide-ranging. The specific details come before the committee and its sub-divisions, who are empowered to call evidence from civil servants and military officials when required.

Owen was not the only communist-orientated MP to sit upon a committee where strategic material was available in such minute detail. No intelligence service could have had a better or more satisfactory channel of information.

Under the definition of 'agents of influence' can also be assigned communist activity within British trade unions and local constituency parties. But for a handful of men such as Frank Chapple, who in 1961 was prepared to endure every sort of mental and physical pressure, communists would have retained the complete domination of Britain's Electrical Trades Union, which is strategically vitally important. As it was, legal action to break that communist stranglehold cost £100,000 ($208,000). To ensure that control, voting ballots were rigged, minor officials intimidated and national officers lied blatantly. Within the electrical union they failed. But in others – the equally important National Union of Mine-workers, for instance – moderate leadership is being replaced gradually by communist influence.

But it is within the politics of Britain that Moscow has achieved its most recent and greatest success. By quiet, assiduous infiltration, local constituencies of the Labour Party came under the control of extreme left-wing officials during 1980. By July 1981, moderate Socialist MP Roy Hattersley tried to sound a warning. 'Our future is in desperate danger,' he said. He added, 'The International Marxists, Workers' Socialist League and other Trotskyite parasites who are feeding off us see their only hope in the collapse of the genuine Labour Party. The communist party – anxious to offer its lethal embrace – has a similar attitude.'

After a further five months of ineffectual dithering, the Labour Party's weak leader, Michael Foot, finally decided there should be an official enquiry into the effects and influence upon the Party of the Trotskyite Militant Tendency, responding to demands from the fifty-five strong Manifesto Group that the organization should be outlawed. The Labour Party concern would appear to be justified. In 1981 the Militant Tendency updated its political manifesto, entitled *British Perspectives*. Against the background of seven local Labour parties deciding to select Militant Tendency advocates as Labour parliamentary candidates in the next election, the manifesto said, 'It is a possibility that the Labour Party will fail to win a majority in the next election, due to the vacillations and hesitations of the leadership of the Labour Party itself. Such an eventuality would push the Labour Party and the unions even more to the left.' The Militant Tendency was dismissive of attempts to expel it from the Labour movement. It said, 'All organizational measures or witch-hunts will fail in their objectives. It is impossible to separate Marxism from the Labour movement because it represents the real interests of the working class.'

In May 1982, the British Security Commission led by Lord Diplock warned of the security threat posed by these new extremist groups. Their aim, the commission said, 'was to overthrow democratic parliamentary government in this country by violent or other unconstitutional means, not shrinking in the case of most extreme groups from terrorism to achieve their aims. Membership of individual groups is small, but for the most part, active and conspiratorial.'

The report, which the Prime Minister, Mrs Thatcher, declined to publish fully, recommends unspecified changes tightening recruitment into Britain's intelligence services but a relaxation of positive vetting at that time applicable to approximately 68,000 people. Although the report was prompted by allegations that the former MI5 director, Sir Roger Hollis, was a KGB agent, the report says that positive vetting should not be automatically applied to the top three ranks of the British intelligence services.

Mirroring concern growing in the United States at the KGB ability to obtain technological secrets, the report said that the commission's chief concern was how vulnerable were secrets stored or processed electronically, particularly in computers into which trained operatives can gain access.

For many in the Labour Party the concern was too late. As

more and more constituency parties came under the sort of extremist domination that insisted MPs obey local rather than national party or personal motivations, the exodus began from the Labour Party. The Social Democrat Party (SDP) was formed. At the time of writing twenty-six sitting MPs had joined the new party. Throughout England Labour councillors changed to the SDP. In the London Borough of Southwark eleven Labour councillors did so because of take-over attempts by what they called 'lunatics, Marxists and anarchists'. It was not only Socialist MPs who joined the Democrats. There were Conservatives, too. It was precisely the sort of situation in which Moscow delights.

The Conservative Party majority is sufficient for it to carry through for its full five-year term of office. But the next General Election in Britain will be a divisive one. The Conservative Party will go to the polls with a record of having tolerated the highest unemployment rate since World War II. At the 1981 Labour Party conference, there was a backlash against the communist left with the expulsion from the National Executive Committee of five extreme left-wingers. But the power remains with the constituency parties and the British electorate is aware of this. The newly formed Social Democrats, with charismatic and publicly recognizable figures such as Roy Jenkins, Mrs Shirley Williams, William Rodgers and Dr David Owen and the support of the hitherto weak third party in British politics, the Liberals, appear like an ice-cream flavour of the month that has not yet been tasted but should be tried. The result is likely to be confusion, a marginally winning party forced into some alignment with another – as happened with the Labour and Liberal Parties under the supposed Socialist government of James Callaghan.

Strong governments frighten Russia. Uncertain ones, like those in Italy since the end of World War II and – until de Gaulle and his successors – those of France, excite it with their weaknesses.

The evidence before the Franks Committee of Sir Martin Furnival Jones was not the only indication of the penetration the KGB had achieved in Britain.

MI5 suborned Oleg Lyalin, a KGB officer operating in

London under the cover of the Soviet trade delegation in Highgate. Lyalin gave details of KGB war contingency plans to sabotage vital communications and strategic centres in Britain – his target was the early warning system at Fylingdales, in Yorkshire – later to be confirmed by Frantisek August. And gradually Lyalin worked his way through the list of Russians on consular or trade attachments in Britain who were engaged in espionage.

In 1971, the KGB recalled Lyalin to Moscow, for reassignment. But Lyalin had fallen in love with Irene Teplyakova, a married secretary at the Soviet legation. After Lyalin's arrest in London, on a drunken-driving charge, the British authorities granted him the asylum he demanded to remain with the woman he loved.

So closely did the Russian hierarchy, through Andropov, monitor the activities of the KGB that the inevitable embarrassment of Lyalin's defection was immediately realized. Brezhnev cut short an Eastern European tour and was met by the then KGB head, Andropov and the rest of the Politburo at Moscow's Vnukovo airport to discuss its implications. A state reception in honour of the visiting Indian premier, Indira Gandhi, had to be postponed.

As a result of Lyalin's information Sir Alec Douglas-Home, the Foreign Secretary in Edward Heath's Conservative Government, expelled ninety diplomats and trade officials and declared that a further fifteen at that time out of the country, predominantly in Russia, would not be allowed re-entry. It was a shock to Moscow similar to that of the ARCOS office raid, forty-four years before. Russia made a token protest, throwing twelve Britons out of Moscow but stopped there because of private warnings given by Sir Alec to Soviet Foreign Minister Andrei Gromyko that if it became a tit-for-tat battle there was sufficient evidence to expel even more of the two hundred Russians remaining in Britain.

Knowledge of at least some of the names of the Russians expelled from Britain indicates the implacable determination of the Soviet Union to infiltrate its agents into the West.

Boris Kolodyazhny was an operative of the GRU and had been First Secretary at the Soviet embassy in Washington from 1958 to 1963. Vladimir Filiatov, attached to the KGB, had served with the Soviet delegation to the United Nations in New York from 1966 until 1967. Anatoli Akimov, a GRU agent, had used the cover of the Soviet trade organization AMTORG in New York from 1962 until 1966. Sergei Golvbev had been attached to the UN delegation in New York first in 1961 and then again from 1963 until 1964. Vsevolod Generalow, a GRU agent, had operated under the cover of air attaché at the Soviet embassy in Washington until he was expelled for espionage and then quite blatantly re-introduced into Britain. Vyacheslav Yasakev, a KGB recruiter, attended Cornell University from 1965 until 1966. Ivan Azarov, a KGB man, had been Third Secretary at the Soviet Embassy in Washington from 1951 until 1954 and then served again, from 1961 until 1962, as Second Secretary. Richard Vayganskas, a KGB spy, had been with the UN Secretariat from 1960 until 1963 and Yemilya Petrovicheva – whose husband was also a KGB man – had been attached to the Washington embassy from 1962 until 1966.

In 1978 the Russians had the audacity to attempt to get Azarov back into America for the third time. The Federal Bureau of Investigation, America's internal security agency, succeeded in blocking his visa. The FBI were more alert than some other counter-espionage agencies. Filiatov became the Soviet ambassador to Gabon. Yuri Kornienko, another of the Russians expelled from Britain, was posted and accepted into Bangladesh. Yevgeni Kutuzov, who had been Third Secretary in London, went to Nigeria and Eduard Ustenko, who had been First Secretary in London, was posted to Sri Lanka.

The immediate years leading up to 1970 had been for British intelligence a period of intensive internal examination and doubt. For five years there had been indications, sometimes contradictory or disjointed, that MI5, the country's counter-espionage arm, had been penetrated by the KGB. By 1970 circumstantial evidence against Sir Roger Hollis, former director of MI5, had grown so strong that he was recalled from the Somerset retirement he was sharing with his second wife and former secretary and questioned by men who had been his intelligence colleagues. The interrogation was inconclusive and in 1973 Hollis died. A year later Lord Trend, former Secretary to the Cabinet, was asked to re-examine all available evidence and give a verdict on Soviet infiltration.

Trend's conclusion was that the evidence was sufficiently strong to suggest that there had been a traitor within the service. But that if a case had been brought against Hollis —unlikely in view of his retirement from any position of security and because of the shattering effect it would have had upon public and international confidence – it would anyway have been insufficient to obtain a conviction against him.

There are two other people who could have provided information to the Russians, apart from Hollis. His deputy, Graham Mitchell, was later cleared during an internal investigation of being one of them. Neither he nor the other person is still in British intelligence.

As early as 1920 the IRA sought assistance from Moscow. Their emissaries arrived with grandiose military titles and initially – just as the Palestinians were to be regarded forty years later – the Russians were dismissive. Today that has changed.

The KGB directly and through its subsidiaries actively supports the IRA against Britain in Northern Ireland. Extensive use is made of Czechoslovakia. Irish gunmen are trained within the country and its airline used for the transportation of arms. In 1971, the Dutch intercepted a consignment of Czech weapons purchased through Omnipol, the Czech intelligence front organization. The Czech airline is a regular carrier of Soviet RPG rocket launchers. And in 1973, when the Irish navy intercepted a gun-running ship off its coast, 250 Kalashnikov rifles were among the five tons of arms and ammunition seized.

Through Tass and *Pravda* correspondents allegedly reporting the troubles, the KGB maintains direct liaison with the IRA. British army and civilian intelligence have file records of meetings between IRA officials and Yuri Ustimenko, accredited to Tass, and *Pravda* reporter Yuri Yasnev.

Cuba is also used by the Russians for their involvement in

Ireland. Training camps have been established in Cuba and its embassy in High Holborn, London, is considered by British intelligence to be the chief conduit – despite the Russian presence in Belfast – between the Soviet Union and the Republicans. High Holborn is kept under permanent and intense security observation by the British. So, too, is the consular section of the Cuban delegation in nearby Grape Street.

In 1974 the Russians found a way, still operating today, to get around the earlier expulsion of more than a hundred of their spies. That year the Labour administration of Harold Wilson, which had succeeded the Conservative government of Edward Heath, negotiated a trade deal with the Soviet Union. Under the deal, Moscow was allowed a multi-million credit allowance. That was not the biggest concession. They were also allowed to introduce inspectors into the British factories supplying the goods Russia was buying. A minister of state at the Foreign Office, Roy Hattersley conceded, 'There is no restriction on the number of inspectors of goods being exported to the U.S.S.R.'

By 1980 sixty-five Soviet officials had been infiltrated into British industry. Fifty-nine were attached to companies in England, three in Northern Ireland, already a focal point of Soviet interest, two in Scotland and one in Wales. The firms included Rolls-Royce, Ferranti, Girling, International Computers, Swan Hunter, Vickers and Wilkinson Sword. Other communist-bloc countries have trade agreements with Britain and they, too, are permitted to have inspectors in the factories. The Foreign Office admits that there is no central registry of those inspectors.

Spying exposures continued in Britain in the 1980s.

In December 1982, Hugo Hambleton, a 60-year-old professor at Laval University, Quebec and a former NATO economics expert, was sentenced to ten-years imprisonment at the Old Bailey for disclosing 'cosmic secrets' to the Russians over a period of thirty years. Hambleton, who had been given immunity from prosecution in return for help by the Canadian authorities but arrested when he arrogantly came to London on holiday, claimed that in 1975 he actually had dinner in

Moscow with the then KGB chief Yuri Andropov. It was a claim doubted by professional intelligence operatives.

In November 1982, the Old Bailey trial of Geoffrey Prime disclosed yet another yawning gap in British counter-espionage. For nearly ten years, from the British government's top secret code-breaking and communications centre at Cheltenham – which works in close cooperation and shares information with the equally secret National Security Agency of the United States – Prime spied for the KGB, and remained completely undetected. It was his chance arrest by ordinary policemen on suspicion of sex offences against young girls, for which he was also jailed, and the finding by his wife of spy equipment beneath their bed that led to his being charged. During his undetected and voluntary career of spying Prime went more than once behind the Iron Curtain, was promoted a colonel in the KGB and offered sanctuary in Russia if he ever wanted to defect. He was jailed for a total of thirty-five years.

The expulsion in 1981 of the Second Secretary at the Soviet embassy, Viktor Lazine, for attempting to establish yet another spy ring disclosed the fact that there is an established day-and-night movie camera and photographic surveillance around Kensington Palace Gardens, where the Russian Legation is located. Such surveillance – like the cell-within-cell construction – is standardized procedure of counter-intelligence agencies against the embassies of countries considered hostile. It takes a minimum of thirty men, changing shifts, appearances, transportation and daily work rosters, to maintain a watch upon *one* suspected spy. With those manpower requirements it is impossible for MI5 satisfactorily to monitor all Russian activities in London. Their agents operate from the consular and embassy premises in Kensington Palace Gardens and from diplomatic addresses in Edith Road and Kensington's Earls Terrace. There is the Soviet trade and diplomatic enclave in West Hill, Highgate. *Soviet News*, *Soviet Weekly* and Novosti Press Agency operate from Rosary Gardens. Aeroflot has offices in Piccadilly, together with management accommodation in Edith Way. Intourist has premises in Regent Street. There is the Russian Narodny Bank in King William Street in the City, London's financial heart. There are also accredited Soviet journalists.

And that is only the basis. From their own embassies, consulates, airlines, travel agencies, trade fronts, press representatives and finance houses operate, on behalf of the KGB, spies from Czechoslovakia, Hungary, Poland, Bulgaria, Cuba and East Germany.

In his evidence to the Franks Committee in 1972, Sir Martin Furnival Jones said, 'There is virtually no information about this country or indeed any other country in the West which they [the Russians] are not anxious to obtain.'

It was an understatement.

CHAPTER SIX

THE INFILTRATION
OF AMERICA AND THE WORLD

Since 1917 the avowed determination of Russia has been, wherever and however, to spread communist domination throughout the world. The KGB is the means used to achieve that ambition. The chief target – called *glavni protivnik* or main enemy – is the United States of America.

A former FBI director, J. Edgar Hoover, once estimated the number of Communist Party members in the United States at 74,000 and then added, 'What is important is the claim of the communists themselves that for every Party member there are ten others ready, willing and able to do the Party's work.'

After America the next targets are NATO and West Germany; and finally the under-developed countries.

As I detail in the following chapter, the spearhead of the spying operations within America is the United Nations, because of the freedom of movement allowed Soviet diplomats and personnel. But there is an awesome back-up. The KGB operates from the antennae- and aerial-haired Soviet embassy, just four blocks away from the White House on Washington's 16th Street. There are twelve separate antennae. There is one for a standard FM radio, an omni-directional high-gain aerial for short-range radio, four log-periodic for VHF television, two microwave receivers of which one is for Home Box Office and the other unknown, one log-periodic low frequency aerial for international radio receiving and transmission, two ultra-high frequencies and another rhombic for international radio transmission and reception. Spying apparatus is already installed in new embassy quarters at Wisconsin Avenue and Calvert Street. The KGB's allied spying organization, the GRU, operates from the offices of the military, air and naval attachés in Belmont Road, Washington. The KGB have agents in the offices of agriculture and irrigation, at Phelps

Place, their information and cultural offices on 18th Street, in the department of their maritime attaché on L Street, in the office of fisheries affairs on Massachusetts Avenue and in the visa and consular office on Decatur Street. There are also operatives working from the Aeroflot offices, even nearer to the White House on 16th Street and installed in the fourth-floor apartment complex occupied by Soviet personnel at 1500 Massachusetts Avenue. There are also thirty-one Soviet journalists accredited to the White House, permitting them off-the-record briefings and knowledge of Senate and Congressional hearings and investigations to which the public have access. Working from the 16th Street embassy is Pavel Bessmertnik. His diplomatic title is minister councillor. In undiplomatic reality, Bessmertnik, a regular party-goer who takes his exercise riding in Rock Creek Park, is a colonel general in the KGB – the highest rank attached to the Washington embassy. He was dispatched specifically by the First Chief Directorate to the American capital to recruit spies and agents of influence for the Soviet Union. He is not, however, nominally in control of KGB activities in Washington. This is the job of the *rezident*, who in Washington is Dimitri Yakushkin.

The spying apparatus of the KGB does not end in Washington. In addition to the capital and to the United Nations there are Soviet consulates in New York and San Francisco, housing agents. San Francisco, strategically placed close to the Mare Island naval base where U.S. submarines are serviced and 'Silicon Valley', where six hundred companies engaged in advanced silicon-chip development for the U.S. government are based, is staffed by over one hundred Russians, 75 per cent of whom are intelligence operatives. Soviet Consul General Aleksandr Chikvaidze was not originally a diplomat: his vocation was that of an engineer. He was once chairman of the Soviet Union's Committee on Science and Technology.

Shortly before he left in April 1982, as the CIA's deputy director, Admiral Bobby Ray Inman warned of a 'haemorrhage of this country's technology' to the Soviet Union. Speaking to two House sub-committees on science and technology, Inman pleaded with scientists voluntarily to censor some of their papers on sensitive technology. He even suggested the American government might impose mandatory restrictions unless there was some voluntary restraint.

In the same month Lawrence J. Brady, assistant U.S. secretary of commerce, told a lunch of the Association of Former Intelligence Officers that the Reagan administration had 'aggressively' imposed restrictions during the previous year of exports to Eastern-bloc countries. Brady said the KGB had built an industrial espionage network of vast proportions, which had 'blanketed the developed capitalist countries . . . sucking up formulas, patents, blueprints and know-how with frightening precision'. Inman said during the House of Representatives hearing that 70 per cent of the 'outflow of technology' came from KGB espionage activities and a proportion of the remaining 30 per cent from the failure of scientists to keep secret their sensitive work.

There is a suspicion among certain former senior counter-intelligence operatives within the CIA that the KGB managed to place an agent within the Agency's headquarters at Langley, Virginia. That suspicion is based upon the de-briefing as long ago as 1961 of Anatoli Golitsin, a KGB major who defected in Finland, denounced Kim Philby and then warned that Moscow intended to attempt an infiltration.

In 1964 Yuri Nosenko was granted asylum in the United States from his UN attachment in Geneva with an apparently priceless offer – he claimed to have been the KGB case officer for Lee Harvey Oswald and to be in a position to prove that the assassin of President Kennedy had no involvement with the Russian intelligence organization during Oswald's defection to Russia from 1959 until his return to the United States in 1962.

The counter-intelligence chief, James Angleton, was one of those who doubted Nosenko, regarding him as a disinformation agent. Angleton's determination to prove his case created friction between him and the then CIA director, William Colby. In 1974, after Angleton had been named in Congressional hearings as head of the department responsible for the illegal opening of American mail, the counter-intelligence chief and a number of his top aides were made to resign. Four years later Nosenko was declared by the CIA to be a 'well-adjusted citizen' and utilized as a consultant.

I was told in 1982 that the counter-intelligence department of the CIA was still weakened by the extent of the 1974 reorganization. Colby told me during a lengthy meeting that he regretted what had happened to Angleton.

After World War II the shocked administrations of Presidents Truman and Eisenhower learned how deep-rooted Soviet penetration was within the American government. Official records show that during and immediately after the war Soviet spies and informants were in position in every strategic government department, leaking to Moscow the innermost secrets and discussions of America's leaders.

In the Office of Strategic Services, the forerunner of what today is the CIA, the Soviet spies were Duncan Lee, Leonard Mins, Julius Joseph and Helen Tennery. David Wheeler operated for Russia from within the counter-intelligence department of the War Department. Within that department itself William Ullmann was a spy. Abraham Silverman leaked secrets of the Air Force. Within the State Department and with access to the cipher room of the Office of Strategic Services operated Robert Miller and Donald Hiss. The Soviet intelligence apparatus had Joseph Gregg, Bernard Redmont and William Park supplying them with information from the department of Inter-American affairs. Norman Buster was in place in the Justice Department. The cell within the Treasury Department was particularly strong. Agents there included Harry Dexter White, Nathan Silvermaster, Harold Glasser, Solomon Adler, William Taylor and Sonia Gold. The infiltration of the Foreign Economic Administration was equally impressive. Spies there were Frank Coe, Allan Rosenberg, Lauchlin Currie, Phillip Keepey, Michael Greenberg and Bela Gold. In the vitally important War Production Board, the cell consisted of Irving Caplan, Victor Perlo, John Abt, Edward Fitzgerald and Harry Magdorf. In the Department of Agriculture – vital to a country never able to produce sufficient foodstuffs for its population – Moscow received information from Harold Ware, Nathan Witt, Lee Pressman, Henry Collins and Bela Gold. Charles Kramer and Victor Perlo operated from the Office of Price Administration.

That was not the complete extent of the penetration.

Investigators found that secrets had been leaked from the White House, six Congressional committees, the office of the Manhattan Project (where the atomic bombs that destroyed Hiroshima and Nagasaki were developed), the National Labor Relations Board, the North Africa Control Board, the Bureau of Standards and Census, the Civil Service Commission, the Offices of Education and War Information, the Federal Housing Administration and the Federal Security Administration, the Government Printing Office, the Library of Congress, the Maritime Labor Board, the National Archives, the National Youth Administration, the Military Government bodies in postwar Germany and Japan, the Railroad Retirement Board, the Reconstruction Finance Corporation, the Resettlement Administration, the Securities and Exchange Commission, the Social Security Administration, the War Manpower Commission, the U.S. War Assets Administration, the War Shipping Administration, the Veterans' Administration, the Tariff Commission, the U.S. Information Board and the United Nations Relief and Rehabilitation Agency.

In 1980 it was discovered that David Barnett, a contract employee for the CIA from 1958 to 1963 and then a full-time employee in the Agency's Directorate of Operations had been paid $85,050 (£45,000) by his Russian controllers, with instructions to infiltrate the Senate Select Committee on Intelligence. That order followed his earlier, unsuccessful, attempt to infiltrate the House Intelligence Committee.

Henry Kissinger, National Security Adviser to President Nixon, has confirmed an open approach from a high-ranking and known KGB agent. It happened in 1968, between the period of Nixon's election and inauguration. The man was named Boris Sedov. Kissinger says that he was visited by Sedov, whom he describes as 'a KGB operative who seemed to have had the Rockefeller assignment during the campaign and who tagged along with me ever since.'

Sedov's mission was to discover if Nixon would be prepared to meet Leonid Brezhnev immediately after the inauguration. Kissinger said he thought it unlikely. During their encounter, according to Kissinger, Sedov kept insisting Nixon should include in his inaugural address something 'to the effect that he was keeping open his lines of communication with Moscow.' Kissinger records, 'I saw no harm in it,' and so it appeared in Nixon's speech.

The Czech defector Frantisek Tisler, who held the rank of lieutenant colonel in the Czech army but served in the Czech embassy in Washington as chief of their military intelligence directorate, described how the Soviet Union employed satellite intelligence organizations.

Tisler recounted, 'This mission called for me to attempt to personally recruit American citizens to act as agents and, in their agent capacity, to furnish me with intelligence on classified materials related to the U.S. military development. The officers of my staff were also engaged in similar operations, although not all of them used the cover of the military attaché's office.'

Tisler, who said his true function was known by the ambassador, claimed 45 per cent of the staff either at the Washington embassy or at their mission at the United Nations in New York were engaged in espionage. He said, 'One of the main reasons for maintaining an embassy is to conduct espionage against the U.S.'

The true extent of that espionage effort was disclosed by another Czech, Joseph Frolik. He itemized the targets of KGB penetration to be every strata and level of American society, from the White House down to small town police forces.

Frolik also disclosed that the KGB ordered utmost surveillance upon American consumer affairs watchdog Ralph Nader, a surveillance so intense that Nader was put under observation by agents when he undertook foreign visits. At Moscow's instructions – because they considered he was a powerful and influential figure in American public life – the Czech service created a detailed file upon Nader, particularly listing his contacts with government agencies, departments and officials of influence or authority. Frolik described the dossier as 'a target file, not an agent file'.

Russia suffered a setback to its espionage activities in America by the defection in 1980 of a KGB colonel whose cover name in the United States was Rudolf Albert Herrmann. He was the highest ranking Soviet spy to be uncovered by the FBI since the 1957 arrest of Colonel Rudolf Abel, later swapped for U-2 pilot Gary Powers. In the event of any diplomatic break between the U.S.S.R. and America, Herrmann would have controlled Russian espionage activities in the United States.

For eleven years Herrmann worked under the cover of a freelance photographer, in reality setting up dead letter boxes for other spies.

He would still have been a Russian agent and a respected and well-liked citizen of Hartsdale, on the outskirts of New York – he lived at 5 Andover Road, in a brown, ranch-style house – had it not been for radioed instructions from Moscow. Herrmann was married; his wife's name was Inger and there were two sons, Peter, aged twenty-one, and Michael, who was fifteen.

The Centre in Moscow decided to make Michael a spy, like his father. Herrmann's orders were to return the boy to the Soviet Union for training. Rather than do that and involve his son in the lifetime of spying that he had known, Herrmann fled. As a result of his debriefing, five diplomats were quietly expelled from America for their spying activities.

The Soviet Union has access to official sources without employing either embassy or UN-installed agents. America allows a surprisingly large number of scientists and technology experts into the country on exchange visits. The flow was supposed to have been halted because of the Soviet invasion of Afghanistan but in the eighteen-month period following that occupation the American State Department granted visas to 470 Soviet experts in advanced technology. They have attended lectures and symposia and have been allowed to put questions and exchange information on lasers, high-energy physics, computers and particle accelerators.

The last subject is of intense interest to the Soviet Union. For good reason. It is the technology involved in the creation and building of what has been referred to as the Domesday Weapon. Soviet experiments are being conducted near the city of Semipalatinsk, northeast of Tashkent. The particle beam weapon is triggered by a controlled nuclear explosion from which giant electrical energy is generated. This is stored for several seconds, then electrons of high energy and intensity are injected into a collective accelerator which takes the pulsed stream of electrons, mixed with heavier protons, and then accelerates them with such velocity that a lightning bolt is created.

All three branches of the American armed forces have been working on the development of such a weapon. The greatest progress has been made at the New Mexico laboratories at Los Alamos, where the atomic bombs of Hiroshima and Nagasaki were created. The project — codenamed Sipapu — has almost reached the point where a vehicle can be launched and a proton beam fired in outer space. A particle beam weapon eviscerates anything at which it is pointed and would render obsolete the current rocket-carried atomic, hydrogen or neutron weaponry upon which America and Russia are depending.

Until that time, however, the Soviet Union is concentrating upon intercontinental ballistic missiles. And again, the United States has helped to make the Soviet development easier. After twelve years of refusal on the grounds that they were strategically vital to the security of America, President Nixon in 1972 agreed, as part of his *détente* programme with Moscow, to the sale — for $20,000,000 (£10,526,315) — of machines which manufacture minuscule ball bearings perfecting the performance of inertial guidance systems for ballistic missiles. Within eight· years, Russia developed the SS-18 multiple warhead rocket with a degree of destructive accuracy that practically makes obsolete America's silo-bound 1054 Minutemen and Titan missiles.

As a result of this Russian development, the administration of President Reagan had to urge the construction — at a cost of $6,196,743,000,000 (£32,787,000,000) — of the MX missile system, which can be constantly transported on moveable tracks from site to site.

The KGB ability to gather scientific information does not finish there. More than eighty Russians were, in 1981, being allowed to study under U.S. government-sponsored exchange programmes. Over thirty were placed for the 1980–81 academic year at the Massachusetts Institute of Technology, Stanford, Northwestern and UCLA.

So concerned are Western intelligence chiefs at the success

of Russian infiltration that in the early part of 1981, Sir Frank Dicks, head of Britain's MI6 and CIA director William Casey held meetings to establish a joint Anglo-U.S. combat force, increasing the liaison between both services to defeat infiltration in both countries.

Canada, with its virtually open border with Russia's main opponent, America, has always been a favoured location with the KGB. This became obvious as early as 1945. On 5 September of that year a Soviet cipher clerk, Igor Sergeievich Gouzenko – so terrified of liquidation that despite plastic surgery he still wears a white hood and speaks through a voice distorting device when appearing publicly – defected from the Russian red-bricked, three-storey embassy in Ottawa's Charlotte Street. With him he took one hundred documents. They proved that the KGB had learned every secret of America's war-time atomic energy programme (the Manhattan Project) through Klaus Fuchs and Alan Nunn May. As well as Canadian spies it identified a seventeen-strong cell in the United States.

Two of these spies, Ethel and Julius Rosenberg, with another cell member, Morton Sobell, were sentenced to death on charges of conspiracy to commit espionage. It was the McCarthy era of American history, with the fear of communism stoked to almost hysterical proportions. Nevertheless, the Rosenberg sentence caused a groundswell of protest throughout the country but it failed to save the couple. Rejecting the Rosenbergs' plea for clemency, at the end of two years of legal wrangling after the sentence, President Eisenhower said, 'I can only say that by immeasurably increasing the chances of atomic war, the Rosenbergs may have condemned to death millions of innocent people all over the world.'

Gouzenko's information provided a fascinating insight into the technical workings of Soviet intelligence – he was the code liaison between Moscow and the GRU *rezident*, Colonel Nikolai Zabotin – and the first mass departure of Soviet diplomats from Canadian territory. More were to follow.

In 1965 Anatoli Bychkov and Vladimir Poluchkin were expelled for attempting to suborn Canadian civil servants. In

1978 eleven Russians were expelled and two in Moscow were told they could not return after two Russians – one of whom was Igor Vartanian, First Secretary at the Soviet mission – approached a member of the Royal Canadian Mounted Police (RCMP) and asked him to provide profiles on other members of the force.

In January 1980, Captain Igor Bardeev, the military, air and naval attaché, Colonel Eduard Aleksanjan, the assistant attaché, and V. I. Sokolov, whose cover was that of an embassy chauffeur, were expelled from Canada after counter-espionage agents discovered their plan to set up a network in the United States. A sum of $94,500 (£50,000) had been budgeted for it.

Rudolf Herrmann, the KGB colonel so important that he was to be entrusted with control of all Soviet intelligence within America if there was ever a diplomatic break, spent six years in Canada before being moved south, into the suburban ranch-style respectability of the United States.

To the delight of Moscow, the Royal Canadian Mounted Police at the end of 1981 was stripped of its responsibility for internal security. A commission of enquiry found that they had abused their investigatory powers over internal dissent among French speakers – particularly in Quebec – who wanted the province to secede. The criticism of the RCMP was severe. The commission found in their 1,800-page indictment that the Mounties considered themselves above the civilian control to which they were properly responsible and because of that contempt had lied to those controllers. The report stated, 'The RCMP, through its recruitment, training and management practices engulfs its members in an ethos akin to that found in a monastery of religious order.' A new internal security body was formed, of course. But there was an inevitable hiatus, precisely the sort of atmosphere the KGB recognizes and utilizes. I have spoken at length to one of the Western world's most experienced counter-espionage experts who estimates that it will be at least five years before Canada's replacement agency will even begin to become effective.

The KGB has created throughout the world a gigantic array

of front organizations behind which it functions and operates.

The World Peace Council, with headquarters in Helsinki, Finland, claims affiliation in more than 130 countries. It was through this organization that the newly elevated Andropov mounted his most successful campaign in the immediate weeks after his succession to absolute power. Within four months of his election, the U.S. State Department estimated that the Soviet Union had spent $600,000,000 (£394,736,000) in the worldwide support of peace movements.

In America President Reagen openly accused Russia of infiltrating peace groups and Edward J. O'Malley, assistant FBI director in charge of the Bureau's intelligence division testified before the House of Representatives Select Committee on Intelligence that KGB officers in the United States had been ordered 'to devote serious attention to the antiwar movement in the United States'. O'Malley said that another communist front, the U.S. Peace Council, was one of the organizers of a huge protest for peace in New York in June 1982.

In England the Conservative Party chairman, Cecil Parkinson accused the Soviet Union of funding world peace movements and alleged communist infiltration of Britain's Campaign for Nuclear Disarmament. In Germany the Greens, a peace party, attained five per cent of the vote in a national election, gaining them 30 seats in the Bundestag. In Britain the link with the World Peace Council is through the British Peace Assembly. The International Institute for Peace, based in Vienna, has member organizations in nine countries other than Austria. The Afro-Asian People's Organization, based in the Egyptian capital of Cairo, has established committees in most Asian and African countries. The World Federation of Trade Unions, in Prague, boasts a membership of 190,000,000. Ninety per cent of that figure refers to workers in communist countries, where any sort of trade union freedom is ludicrous, but 190,000,000 is still an impressive figure. The World Federation of Democratic Youth, in the Hungarian capital of Budapest, claims a membership of 150,000,000 in 110 countries. There are 118 member organizations, with a total of ten million members, forming the International Union of Students, based in the Czechoslovakian capital of Prague.

The Women's International Democratic Federation, from its East Berlin headquarters, lists a membership of two hundred million. The International Organization of Journalists, with offices in Prague, represents 150,000 influence- and opinion-forming members in 112 countries. From its Brussels base, the International Association of Democratic Lawyers attests a membership of 25,000 in fifty-seven countries. No membership figures are published for the Christian Peace Conference, administered from Prague, but the affiliation is throughout forty-eight countries. The International Federation of Resistance Fighters, in Vienna, counts a membership of five million throughout twenty-two countries and the World Federation of Scientific Workers, in Paris, boasts a 400,000 membership from thirty-one countries, with the addition of corresponding members in a further twenty-six countries.

Since the end of World War II, America has spent billions of dollars trying to prevent Leftist governments becoming established in Europe. There was concern, therefore, at the 1981 election in France of the Socialist President, François Mitterand, and the appointment into his cabinet of four communists. The concern is not that such appointments indicate obvious security dangers, rather that there is an administration – no matter how apparently independent – more favourably inclined towards Moscow.

For more than thirty years, France has been fertile ground for the Soviet intelligence services. The first resident espionage director settled in Paris in 1925 and since then, despite periodic arrests and show trials, the Russians have established cells throughout the country. Numerically the Communist Party of France has always been the strongest national party outside Russia, although there have been repeated efforts to make it appear that it remains independent of Moscow's control, which is untrue. Immediately after World War II that strength resulted in Communists holding major government positions. Before the war Moscow had established in France an organization called Workers Correspondents – Rabcors – supposedly to enable journalists to provide news for Russian newspapers. In reality, they were espionage fronts. Within three years of the war ending, 650 Rabcors were established within the Paris area, with a further 200 spread throughout the country. So easy was France regarded as an espionage base that Paris was the first headquarters for the World Federation of Democratic Youth, the World Federation of Democratic Women and the World Federation of Trade Unions. It was not until 1951 that all three were expelled.

France became an important target for Soviet intelligence with the original establishment there of NATO. In 1952 two Soviet networks were smashed – one in Lyon and one in the capital – and from the material seized during the arrests it became clear that nearly every French military secret had been passed to Russia. Also found was a map plotting the majority of NATO sites on French territory. In Toulon another cell was found to contain members of the French police and naval security officers and today Western intelligence believe that French police are heavily infiltrated – one estimate goes as high as 30 per cent – by communists and agents spying for the Soviet Union.

The level of Russian penetration in France was disclosed in 1954. That year, two officials, René Turpin and Roger Labrusse, of the top-secret Committee for National Defence were arrested and charged with supplying secret military documents to a Communist agent, André Baranes. Within weeks of the start of the investigation, the Secretary General of the Defence Committee, Jean Mons, was arrested and accused of having damaged state security by passing on secrets. The information had been handed to Jacques Duclos, chairman of the Politburo of the French Communist Party –and longtime Moscow agent – by Jean Dides, a police inspector.

In France, as in every other country, the KGB utilized the services of its satellites and by 1971 an official of the French counter-espionage organization estimated that of the one thousand Communist representatives accredited, and therefore known to the authorities, at least six hundred were professional spies. That same year French counter-intelligence arrested Dmitri Volokov, who, under questioning, admitted passing to the Russians over a period of ten years every technical detail of the French atomic energy programme that had come into his possession.

During the immediate post-war confusion of a divided country, the Soviet Union established a massive and effective spy organization in West Germany and it continues to regard the country as one of its most important bases. In East Germany there exists the biggest KGB headquarters outside Moscow. Defector Aleksei Myagkov told West German intelligence debriefers in 1976 that from its Potsdam Directorate the KGB controls 1,200 officers engaged solely in espionage against West Germany, because of the opportunity in that Warsaw frontline country to spy upon NATO. Within the country itself, counter-espionage chiefs admitted, also in 1976, that there were 10,000 spies or informers providing information to Communist controllers. Again, satellite services are as active as the Russians. So successful have the Russians been that there can be few intelligence secrets passing through Bonn in the last thirty-seven years that have not found their way on to a desk in Dzerzhinsky Square.

In 1974 it was discovered that Günther Guillaume, personal assistant to West German Chancellor Willy Brandt, was an East German intelligence officer. This meant that throughout Brandt's period of office, which ended with his abrupt resignation in embarrassment at the disclosure, *every* secret had been passed on to Moscow. Guillaume, who was jailed, was released as part of a prisoner-for-refugee exchange in September 1981.

Guillaume was the Soviet's second, and more successful, effort to gain access to Brandt's office. In 1966, when Brandt was West Germany's Foreign Minister, the Russians attempted to have appointed as his secretary a deceived and manipulated girl named Leonore Sutterlin. Six years earlier she had married an East German spy, Heinz Sutterlin. At his prompting, and under threat of losing him, she began to steal secrets from the Foreign Ministry, where she was a secretary. Her application to join Brandt's staff failed. Leonore was still, however, extraordinarily useful.

The control for both her and her husband was Yevgeni Runge, who defected to America in 1968 and who gave evidence before a Senate investigatory committee in 1970. He said that from the Foreign Ministry Leonore supplied almost three thousand documents to Moscow, of which nearly one thousand had either top secret or secret classification. 'We read the reports of diplomatic couriers from abroad mostly even before German Foreign Minister Schröder got them,' testified Runge.

Even earlier, in the 1950s, the Czech service recruited a member of the Bundestag, Alfred Frenzel, who sat on the West German Defence Committee. Frenzel's case officer was Ladislav Bittman, who defected to the West after the Soviet invasion of Czechoslovakia in 1968. Bittman told American intelligence officers, 'We knew exactly what the West Germans were discussing as far as the defence system of West Germany was concerned.' Frenzel was arrested in 1960 and jailed for seventeen years, the longest sentence imposed in West Germany since World War II.

In 1966 the Czechs recruited West German Admiral Luedke and the deputy chief of West Germany's intelligence directorate, General Wendland. Both committed suicide when investigations began into their activities.

A particular target of the KGB in West Germany is the Munich-based American propaganda outlet, Radio Free Europe; unquestionably, from my enquiries, it was Georgi Markov's employment by RFE that cost him his life. After his defection, Joseph Frolik told U.S. senators that the communist authorities regarded Radio Free Europe as a great irritant. 'It constantly evokes fits of anger among the leading representatives of communist regimes,' he testified.

Frolik added, however, that during his period as an intelligence officer with the Czech secret service, the Minister of the Interior Rudolf Barak claimed that the communists had so successfully infiltrated the broadcasting station that they were able to use it to transmit coded messages to their agents in the field. Frolik identified one Czech-controlled KGB infiltrator as George Salmon Ngugi Munua, codenamed George, a nephew of the late Kenyan President Jomo Kenyatta.

Frolik said in further evidence that before the KGB decided to use the Washington-financed radio station for their own purposes, the Czech Interior Minister Barak considered blowing it up and that a plan was considered by Major Jaraslav Nemec (alias Nekola), the Czech vice-consul in Salzburg, to poison its staff. Nemec's proposal was to put atropine, an alkaloid derivative of deadly nightshade, into the salt shakers in the RFE cafeteria. In small amounts, atropine is an hallucinogen and in large quantities, it can kill. Frolik says that the plan misfired because the Czech agent to whom Nemec gave his instructions was a double for the CIA and informed the station controllers. An arrest warrant was issued for Nemec, who was smuggled out of the country in the boot of a car.

During 1973, the Soviet Union registered six shipping and transport companies in West Germany, with affiliated offices in Holland and Belgium. It has long been known that the Soviet trawler fleets are constructed entirely for spying, not fishing: Soviet naval commander, Captain Nikolai Fedorovich Artamonov testified before the Committee on UnAmerican Activities that the refrigerated holds of the trawlers were filled with fish *before* they left their Russian ports. The purpose of the transportation companies can be gauged from the discovery that the KGB had evolved 'land trawlers'. Electronically packed juggernaut lorries have been detected by Scandinavian counter-intelligence crossing from the Soviet Union into Finland. They drive from Finland through Sweden and Denmark and then cross by ferry into East Germany. The Soviet juggernauts, like others operating through Europe, carry an international TIR carnet enabling them to pass unchecked through customs checks at borders.

Italy, like France, has a large and impressive Communist Party: in 1952 it was disclosed that even the Vatican had been penetrated when Father Aligheri Tondi, a professor at the Gregorian Academy, was identified as a KGB agent.

In 1965, following Moscow instructions, eight members of the Italian Communist Party travelled to Prague, as guests of the Czech government. They promptly had to surrender their passports, which were doctored and then used by Czech espionage agents on hurried trips abroad.

There is overwhelming evidence that the assassination attempt upon Pope John Paul II in St Peter's Square on

13 May 1981 – 'an act of war in times of peace' according to Italy's Defence Minister Lelio Lagorio – was organized by the KGB with the assistance of the ever-obedient Bulgarian Secret Service.

Signor Francesco Mazzola, the Italian junior minister in charge of security forces at the time of the attempt says so publicly. So, too, does Dr Ilario Martella, the Italian public prosecutor investigating the Moscow link. Former U.S. Secretary of State Henry Kissinger says CIA sources – one of whom he names as Richard Helms, the Agency's one-time Director – have convinced him the Russians were involved. Colonel Stefan Svredlev, former head of the Bulgarian service who defected to the West in 1979 says he has no doubt that the organization he once controlled was involved 'but they did it on the instructions of the KGB.'

The evidence created a diplomatic dilemma for the West. Andropov, then the Soviet leader with whom the Western leaders had personally to deal, was in charge of the KGB at the time of the assassination attempt and approved it. To spare their President the difficulty of meeting a man who mounted the attempt, the CIA officially produced a fence-sitting analysis that although the KGB and the Bulgarian service knew in advance an attempt would be made they did not interfere because they regarded the would-be assassin as a 'known crazy' unlikely to succeed.

The 'known crazy', however, came close to succeeding. Mehmet Ali Agca – already a convicted murderer who had escaped from jail – shot the Pope in the stomach, shoulder and left hand. At his trial Agca claimed to have acted alone. Only when he was sentenced to life imprisonment in the impregnable Ascoli Piceno jail – the first year in solitary confinement – did Agca change his story. He was, he told Italian security men, working with Bulgarians. One he named as Ivanov Antonov, head of the Rome offices of Balkan airlines and someone who accompanied him on planning visits to St Peter's Square. Antonov was arrested and charged with 'active complicity' in the attack upon the Pope. Another person identified by Agca was Teodorov Ajvazov, chief accountant at the Bulgarian Embassy in Rome, whom Agca claims was next to him in St Peter's Square when he made the attempt and another who accompanied him, with Antonov, on reconnaissance visits before the actual shooting. Ajvazov, whom Agca says carried disorientating percussion granades to assist in the attack but never used them, fled back to Sofia before he could be detained.

An amateur photographer took a picture at the moment of the attack upon the Pope showing a man other than Agca wielding a gun. He was subsequently identified as Omer Ay, arrested in Hamburg in 1982 and currently facing extradition application from Turkey, where he is wanted in connection with two separate killings.

A third Bulgarian implicated by Agca was Bekir Celenk, an arms dealer and drug trafficker whom Agca says offered him $1,060,000 (£500,000) to kill the Pope. Celenk and Ajvazov were produced by the Bulgarian government at a Sofia press conference to deny the allegations of complicity in the plot against the Pope.

The motive for the attack was Poland. The Pontiff had publicly received the Polish Solidarity leader Lech Walesa – himself a target of assassination planning during his visit to Rome – in a Vatican audience. The meeting backed the dissent the trade union was creating within Poland. Further, at the time the Soviet Union were considering armed intervention within the country, the Pope wrote personally to the then Soviet leader Leonid Brezhnev threatening to resign the papacy and return to stand 'shoulder to shoulder with my Polish brothers' at the first indication of military intervention.

The Italian Defence minister Lagorio told the Italian parliament, 'The assassination of the charismatic figure of the Pope was an alternative solution to a project of a military invasion of Poland.'

It was a further seven months before Russia orchestrated the moves to regain the control over Poland it feared it was losing at the height of Solidarity's popularity. American intelligence officers to whom I have spoken believe that Moscow and the KGB were directly behind the martial law decree by the Polish military. After initial hesitation other Western intelligence services concurred with that view. There were reports, unconfirmed but persistent, that in the immediate dates prior to the army move on 12 December 1981, the then KGB chief Andropov was in Warsaw. Within five days of the take-over he was certainly in the Hungarian capital of Budapest, monitoring the possibility of dissent spreading throughout the Eastern bloc. The martial law decree was printed in the Soviet Union. And from the Soviet Union came the electronic jamming of the BBC Polish broadcasts, preventing the population hearing truthful reports of what was happening in their country, leaving them only the military controlled and censored television and radio transmissions for information.

After Agca's escape from the supposedly top-security Kartel Maltepe jail – where he was serving a sentence for the murder of Abdi Ipekci, the editor-in-chief of the Turkish independent newspaper *Millivet* – Vatican and West German intelligence investigations concluded that the Turkish secret police had been infiltrated by the KGB.

Following that escape Agca moved rapidly throughout Europe, finally coming to Bulgaria. He was already a trained terrorist and a proclaimed revolutionary, a member of an organization known as the Grey Wolves and alleged to be right wing. It is not. Turkish extremists – posing as Islamic fundamentalists, a movement actively utilized by the KGB – are trained in terrorism by a splinter group of the Popular Front for the Liberation of Palestine. That group is headed by Wadi Haddad, a KGB agent. Agca was instructed by Haddad's organization, briefly in the Lebanon but for a longer and more intensive period in Libya.

In Bulgaria Agca was befriended by an arms dealer colleague of Bekir Celenk, a man named Omer Mersan. It was Mersan, whose arms and drugs deals are approved by the Bulgarian intelligence service for the currency they generate, who provided Agca with a false passport which enabled him to move freely back into Europe and into Italy. That passport was made by the Bulgarian Secret Service. Agca also had meetings in the Bulgarian capital of Sofia and Vitosha – a place once well known to Georgi Markov – with a Bulgarian named Mustafa Eof. Signor Mazzola, the Italian junior minister, has established links between Eof and the Bulgarian Secret Service.

Unquestionably the highlight of 1981 for the Kremlin and its neighbouring KGB headquarters in Dzerzhinsky Square was the assassination of Egyptian President Anwar Sadat. In the immediate aftermath of the murder, Israel – whose unbending intransigence over West Bank settlement and Jerusalem greatly contributed to Sadat's internal and external problems – and the Egyptian leader's named successor, Vice-President Hosni Mubarak, declared that the peace accord negotiated between Sadat and Israel's Menachem Begin would survive. The Russian – and therefore that of the KGB – determination is that it should not.

In the overly fulsome panegyrics that immediately followed Sadat's death, he was hailed as a paragon of peace. It was, as I say, overly fulsome. Sadat came to peace late. In 1946 he was a terrorist, accused with others of killing leading Egyptian politician Amin Osman. He tried – and failed – to kill Nahhas Pasha, leader of the Wafd, a nationalist party.

Like many politicians, Sadat was an opportunist. During World War II he considered it opportune to offer to work for the Nazis and was imprisoned by the British for this reason. After succeeding President Nasser in 1970 he considered it opportune as the leader of an impoverished country to court the maniacally unpredictable but immensely rich President Gaddafi of Libya only to quarrel and end up as hated enemies. In 1973, to restore Egyptian pride after the débâcles of previous encounters with Israel, he decided that it was opportune to launch a war – in conjunction with Syria – against Israel which briefly won him control of the Suez Canal and a large proportion of the Sinai beyond. It was a short-lived victory, before his forces were driven back by Jewish counter-attacks. Sadat then considered it opportune to recognize Israel and negotiate peace.

In this, on the surface, he was more successful than with anything he had ever attempted before. His stature immediately rose to that of an international statesman, in which he revelled, with trips to Washington and then, showing an impetuous bravery that was never lacking, actually to Jerusalem and talks with Begin and Israeli leaders. Moscow does not want a peace of Washington's mediation in the Middle East. And Sadat knew that.

Upon Nasser's death he had inherited a country $884,000,000 (£37,000,000) in debt to Moscow, infested with

Soviet technicians and advisers and with a cabinet, armed forces and even intelligence service penetrated to command level by the KGB. Sami Sharaf, head of the Mabahes, the country's counter-espionage service, answered to Dzerzhinsky Square, not Sadat.

Within a year, Sadat arrested ninety communist-controlled conspirators – Sharaf among them – who had been planning to overthrow him; so seriously did Moscow regard his anti-Soviet outburst that President Nikolai Podgorny flew to Cairo to placate him. Sadat, ever the opportunist, assured Moscow of continued friendship and Podgorny, for his part, assured Sadat of Russia's support.

The now loyal Mabahes and the country's external intelligence agency, the Mukhabarat, reported to Sadat within months that the Russian overthrow plans were still being fomented. Sadat's response in July 1972 was to expel 20,000 Russians from his country and look to the West.

After the tripartite English-French-Israeli disaster of the Suez invasion of 1956, quickly followed by the Western withdrawal of funding for the Aswan High Dam – a gap they hurriedly filled – Russia had come to regard Egypt as the base from which it could initiate unrest throughout the Middle East. Sadat's 1972 expulsion shocked them. His visit to Jerusalem in 1977 appalled them. There were still 1,500 Russians in Egypt – ostensibly engineers and technicians but in reality more than one thousand were KGB personnel – and from Moscow came the instructions to mount again the overthrow that had been thwarted five years earlier.

There was sufficient internal dissent upon which the KGB could capitalize. Internationally Sadat was a man of peace and justice; internally he ruled autocratically, allowing no opposition. The KGB – who despite belief to the contrary have involved themselves heavily in Iran – used the religious success in overthrowing the Shah to incite Moslem fundamentalists in Egypt. They influenced Christian Coptics, too, to demand more freedom.

Sadat carried out widespread arrests among religious leaders and then moved against the Russians. He expelled all of the remaining 1,500; the Soviet ambassador, Vladimir Polyakov, was given forty-eight hours to leave Egypt and a

Hungarian diplomat was also declared *persona non grata*.

Reporting on the cabinet meeting at which the decision was taken, the deputy premier, Fuad Moheiddin, said, 'Certain elements in the Soviet Union got in touch with communist elements and made plans to stir sectarian strife and internal sedition as part of a large Soviet scheme for the whole area and especially Egypt.' An official statement declared, 'The Soviet aim was to carry out a hostile plot against the regime, Egypt's national unity and its social security.' The plans had been made and they were too well established.

On 7 October 1981, Sadat attended a military parade in Cairo to celebrate the crossing of the Suez Canal in 1973. During the parade soldiers suddenly sprinted on a suicide mission to kill him. Opportunist to the last, Sadat stood to confront them, believing his charisma would halt them. It did not.

When he inherited Nasser's presidency, Sadat was an unknown man, given only a few months in office by the sceptics. He lasted for eleven years and took the first steps to peace in the Middle East. His successor, the Moscow-trained Mubarak, is known better in the West than in the Arab world. He has been called a strong man who can continue the journey. History could repeat itself but the KGB is unlikely to allow it to do so. A more likely outcome will be that the area reverts to uncertainty and instability, and that is a classic scenario in any part of the world that Russia seeks to influence or dominate. Within three months of Sadat's death came indications that Moscow's bruised influence was being re-established, with the news from Cairo that Russian technicians were being invited back into the country to work once more upon the Russian-built Aswan dam. With them went the KGB.

Egypt is not the only country in the Middle East where the Russians seek to establish themselves. Beirut in the Lebanon has long been a base. In 1980, thirty-seven of the eighty-eight Russians attached to their embassy there were identified as KGB operatives. Ambassador Aleksandr Aleksayevich Solda-tov was the direct link with Yasser Arafat's Palestine Libera-tion Organization. Soldatov is a career intelligence officer and in 1968 he served in Cuba, infiltrating Castro's intelligence organization and binding it even closer to Moscow. First Secretary in the Lebanese embassy in 1980 was Boris Netrebsky, expelled as a spy from Holland in May 1970.

It was in the Lebanon in 1967 that the KGB evolved a plan to assassinate the French President, General de Gaulle, by bombing the route his car was to take through Beirut. The intention was that the assassination would be made to look like the combined assault of the CIA and the Israeli intelligence service, the Mossad.

The Czech intelligence chief in Beirut, Miroslav Jansky-Jarolim, was ordered to find the route de Gaulle's car would be taking and select a site upon that route where the bomb could most effectively be planted. The assassination attempt was cancelled at the last moment because it was decided that it was impracticable.

By 1967, just one year after the decision to make Beirut an important base, the KGB had an agent in place within the American embassy, leaking all the operational bulletins circulating within the building. It installed agents in the American University on recruiting missions and used the Lebanese capital as a gateway for movements of agents into both Africa and South America.

Initially the KGB was dismissive of the Palestinian liberation movements. Today the Palestine Liberation Organization is accorded diplomatic recognition in Moscow. The KGB's attitude changed after the 1967 war between Israel and the Arab nations. Through the Czech embassy links were established with Shafik Alhout, an aide to Yasser Arafat. Agreement was reached to supply the organizations with weapons, and training schools were established, both in Czechoslovakia and Cuba, where the Palestinians could be taught sabotage and subversion.

It was during the 1967 war that the French-built Mirage III-E interceptor plane proved itself better than the supposedly more advanced Soviet MIG. Through a KGB intermediary, in 1969, the Russians approached a Lebanese fighter pilot, Lieutenant Mahmoud Mattar, offering $3,000,000 (£1,250,000) if Mattar would deliver a Mirage into Soviet hands. During Mattar's first meeting with the GRU agent, Vladimir Vasilyev, the sum was reduced to

$2,000,000 (£833,333). At a subsequent encounter with the GRU controller in Beirut, Aleksandr Komiakov, it was agreed that before Mattar took off on a training flight during which he was to radio that he was in trouble and disappear, to fly to Baku in Soviet Azerbaijan, he would be paid 10 per cent of the $2,000,000 (£833,333). The payment was arranged to take place on 3 October 1969. As Komiakov was handing over the $200,000 (£83,333) drawn against the Narodny Bank in Moscow, Lebanese security men, with whom Mattar had all along been co-operating, burst into the apartment. Both Russians were badly wounded in the gun battle that ensued. At first Lebanon refused to allow the two Russians to be freed under diplomatic privilege, but under pressure from Russian-influenced governments of other Arab states, finally capitulated and allowed them to be repatriated to Moscow.

One of those nations who put pressure on Lebanon was Syria, where the KGB had become firmly entrenched. Bakalar Abdul al-Barri, chief of the office of the Syrian prime minister, was suborned and the Syrian counter-intelligence chief, Colonel Jundi, recruited as an agent. The Ba'ath Party was heavily penetrated.

In an effort to weaken future President Assad, then Minister of Defence but clearly an emerging power within the government, the KGB had Jundi organize sabotage raids against the oilfields of neighbouring Iraq, hoping to embroil Assad in a dispute with a fellow Arab state. Iraq's reaction was to believe that it was under the threat of serious aggression and to turn to Moscow for arms. Presented with another client state in the Middle East, the Russians supplied the arms and with them advisers who immediately set about creating spy cells within the country. They still exist today. The Soviet influence has been well established. After French technicians rebuilt the nuclear reactor destroyed by the surprise low-level Israeli air raid in June 1981, Baghdad sought defence aid from Moscow. The response was immediate. Placed around the installation were SAM missiles to prevent either high- or low-level air assault and batteries of 23 millimetre ZSU-23 four-barrelled guns. These guns, directed by radar, can hit low- or medium-attack planes with devastating accuracy. The entire system is under complete Soviet control and that

Russian contingent included both GRU and KGB officers. Syria, too, is dependent upon Moscow for weaponry and missiles.

There has been a political advantage for the Soviet Union in their mistaken invasion of Afghanistan, where Moscow has 80,000 conventional combat troops locked into a war with unconventional guerrilla fighters.

From the CIA, President Reagan has analysis reports of growing Soviet influence in the Persian Gulf, where Kuwait has already established diplomatic relations with Moscow and where the Arab Emirates, Bahrain and Saudi Arabia are openly considering improved relations. America saw the Afghanistan invasion further threatening the strategically important oil-exporting route of the Persian Gulf. Reagan's response was to promise to sell Saudi Arabia the latest technologically developed aerial reconnaissance planes, AWACs, and to move into the area a rapid deployment troop force. The diplomatic reaction was varied. Israel, predictably, protested at once, claiming its safety would be endangered by such aircraft in an Arab country and the Arab nations America is so anxious not to upset resented the implication that they were unable to safeguard their own security and criticized the American administration for its presumption.

The KGB has infiltrated Africa from the Mediterranean in the north to Cape Town on the South Atlantic coast. Although its successes have been impressive it has also had failures, largely from an inherent race consciousness from which it frequently underestimates black Africans. As always, Moscow's ambition is communist domination of other countries. But in Africa, Soviet interest is dictated by the mineral deposits in that continent.

Despite the religious fanaticism of Libya and of President Gaddafi in particular, the Russians have infiltrated the country heavily. In neighbouring Sudan, in 1971, Russia based an abortive coup against President Gaafar Nimeri upon inflated reports of pro-Soviet, anti-government feeling. Nimeri expelled the Soviet ambassador, executed fourteen involved Sudanese and threw out hundreds of Russian and Bulgarian advisers. Throughout 1980 and 1981, with typical labyrinthine intrigue, the Russians were involved on *both* sides of Ethiopia's war with seceding Eritrea and in Somalia, too, in its conflict with Ethiopia. The Soviet Union has poured massive financial aid into Ethiopia and at least two thousand Russian military advisers, both GRU and KGB. In February 1982, the Eritrean People's Liberation Front claimed the Ethiopian government and these Soviet advisers were using the nerve gases Soman and Tabun, dropped from helicopter gunships and MIG 23 bombers.

A communist leader and government are in power in the islands of the Seychelles, important because of their position from which the Indian Ocean can be monitored. Although their strength has been diminished since Arap Moi succeeded Kenyatta as President of Kenya, the Russians have well-established cells in that country, just as they have in Tanzania, despite the friendship of President Nyerere with Peking.

With Tanzania, the Seychelles government has evolved a cynical method of remaining in office. At the age of eleven, male children of the island's politicians – who could plot its overthrow just as they plotted that of the previous President, James Mancham – are expected to spend two years in Tanzania, being politically educated. The effect is to make them hostages to their parents' loyalty. And when they return after two years, the children *are* communists.

From the Maputo capital, a Marxist government is firmly in control of Mozambique and it was from here – and from Zambia in the north – that the Russians trained the black guerrillas during the Zimbabwe fight for independence against white premier Ian Smith.

It was from the Mozambique port of Maputo that the Russians completed the chain of naval stations enabling them to keep fleets of Russian ships in permanent position around the oil routes from the Persian Gulf to the West. In Mozambique there is now installed a floating dock sufficiently sophisticated to carry out underwater repairs to submarines, frigates and destroyers. In addition to the Mozambique facility the Russians have dock facilities in the Dhalek islands, off Ethiopia and submarine-refitting pens in Aden.

Russia pledged full military support to the Patriotic Front

in what was then called Rhodesia if the London peace negotiations failed. In 1979, the Patriotic Front temporarily withdrew from the London talks. Immediately Moscow assured the Zimbabwe African People's Union, ZAPU, that it would provide whatever military aid was necessary to achieve a military victory if the Patriotic Front maintained their boycott. The Soviet advisers warned the ZAPU leaders that various front-line states surrounding them might press for an agreement, for their own immediate benefit. If ZAPU rejected the British proposals, said the Russians, they were ready to back them throughout the fighting.

In November 1979 squads of GRU officers flew into the Zambian capital of Lusaka, to train senior army officers of the Zimbabwe People's Revolutionary Army in covert political action. The course included briefings on how to recruit agents of influence able to subvert legal balloting, the recruitment of agitators and the use of money to disrupt opposition access to the polls. When the election took place, independent observers declared that it was freely conducted. Robert Mugabe, who became the country's Prime Minister, is a communist.

Twice – the first time in 1963 and then again in 1970 – KGB officers have been expelled from Zaire for attempting to organize coups against the government.

In Ghana, to the north, in 1962 the Russians established a focal point for their activities throughout the entire continent, upon the promise to keep President Kwame Nkrumah in power. From the Ghanaian capital of Accra, Russian-trained agents were sent into the Cameroons, the Ivory Coast, Upper Volta, Niger, Togo, Chad, Nigeria, Sierra Leone, Liberia, Gambia, Swaziland, Malawi, Mali, Burundi, Guinea, Rwanda and Portuguese Guinea. The infiltration continued for four years, until anti-communist elements in the army staged a coup while Nkrumah was visiting China. Eleven KGB officers occupying Nkrumah's offices were executed. The government which succeeded Nkrumah published a White Paper, based upon seized records, disclosing the extent of the Russian domination of Ghana and of its use against other African states.

Employing the well-established practice of utilizing satellites, Moscow has conducted the war in Angola largely through Cubans, but during incursions by South African troops Russian military advisers have been captured. Intelligence analysts estimate there are more than one thousand Russians operating in Angola.

To the south, in Namibia, the Russians are supporting the South West Africa People's Organization, SWAPO, in its war with South Africa, a conflict which Western diplomats are fearful could end with an extension of Soviet influence within the continent.

The defection from the Soviet embassy in Canberra in 1954 of Vladimir Petrov disclosed the importance Moscow attaches to infiltration into Australia. Petrov, like Gouzenko in Canada, took with him documentation showing the extent of KGB activities throughout a country seen as pivotal in the Far East and Asia. Petrov testified before an Australian Royal Commission that 'all Tass journalists in Australia are spies.'

Particular attention is paid by the Russians in Australia to Eastern European immigrants. For a period before his defection, Petrov was Third Secretary in charge of the consulate to which immigrants settled in Australia would come to make enquiries about their native countries. That initial enquiry would make the man or woman a subject for Soviet pressure, particularly if he had a relative in the Soviet Union or any of the satellite countries. In addition to Petrov's index, any letters sent from Australia to people living within Russia were opened before delivery, so that an Australian identity and address could be listed and then given to Russians sent specially from Moscow on recruitment missions to Australia.

The cell which Petrov exposed – his wife Yevdokia was also an agent – was only one of several that existed and still exists within Australia. Counter-intelligence discovered evidence, for instance, of Russian attempts to infiltrate uranium-mining companies at Edith River and Radium Hill which Petrov knew nothing about. And in 1981 Australian counter-intelligence investigated, without success, suspicions that a Soviet informant was deeply embedded within the government in Canberra.

Nineteen eighty-one, the year that began so well for the KGB, ended on the same note.

Moscow has always recognized the strategic importance in the Mediterranean of Greece and Turkey, particularly NATO-allied Turkey through whose Bosphorus waterway the Soviet fleets sail to their warm-water ports.

Greece and Turkey are enemies; Greece has a frontier with communist Bulgaria staffed only by customs officers while its army faces Turkey. The KGB has done its best to exacerbate the emnity. Its disinformation department forged documents under the name of President Carter which were critical of both governments, thus trying to worsen their relationship.

The Greek elections of October 1981 provided the KGB with a further opportunity to undermine the Western-orientated attitude of Greece. Through a shell company, the KGB financed a newspaper named *Ethnos*, meaning nation, and created a circulation of 300,000. Its avowed support was for the communist party – KKE – which lost the election. But with its typical caution of backing every horse in the race, Moscow also supported the successful Panhellenic Socialist Movement – Pasok – of Andreas Papandreou.

Though not as satisfying as a communist victory would have been, Pasok's election was good enough. Although somewhat ambivalent, Papandreou's international pledges were to take Greece out of NATO and of the European Common Market. Weakening and increasing the uncertainty of both is a primary aim of the KGB.

The Vietnam war gave the Soviet Union its opportunity to penetrate Asia completely. Throughout the conflict Russia supported the North Vietnamese and that support has continued since the communist victory in 1975. In 1981 American intelligence estimated it was costing Moscow $3,000,000 (£1,538,461) a day to finance Vietnam and its invasion into Cambodia. And Washington, who scarred the country with the defoliant, Agent Orange, and which has been accused of causing physical deformities in children by using the chemical, counter-charge that the Russians used Cambodia to test germ weapons.

Moscow receives what it considers good value for its financial outlay. During its period in the country, America created superbly equipped airfields, particularly at Danang and Tan Son Nhut, in what was Saigon but is now called Ho Chi Minh City. From both these bases Russian TU95 reconnaissance planes blanket Asia on round-the-clock spying missions. American intelligence have abundant evidence of this; the Soviet flights have been detected and monitored by U.S. supersonic spy planes.

Through its foothold in Cuba – the KGB completely dominates Castro's intelligence organization – the KGB has infiltrated throughout Latin America, and uses the apparent refugee line from Havana to the Florida coast, only ninety miles away, as a route to smuggle illegals into the United States of America.

The CIA identified Nicaragua as a staging post for Cuban-fronted infiltration into the South American continent early in 1981. In March 1982, the administration of President Reagan took the unprecedented step of having the then deputy chief of the CIA, Admiral Inman, host a press conference at which he and John Hughes, deputy director of the Defence Intelligence Agency, produced aerial reconnaissance photographs of what they claimed to be Nicaraguan military installations constructed to Cuban design, airfields with runways lengthened to handle Soviet MIG jets and Soviet tanks and artillery in place at some of the installations. At the same time, Reagan approved a $19,000,000 (£10,555,550) CIA covert military operation to build up, with U.S. advisers, a 500-strong Latin American force to operate out of commando camps spread along the Nicaraguan-Honduran border.

American concern in early 1982 was focused on the elections in San Salvador, in which the Americans backed the Christian Democratic party of President José Napoleón Duarte. As has happened so often in the past during American involvement in the politics of Latin America, their backing was a disaster. Duarte obtained the plurality of votes but was defeated by a group of Right-wing parties which formed a coalition to govern. The group was led by Roberto d'Aubuisson, a cashiered army major believed responsible for death-squad murders, including the assassination in 1980 of Archbishop Oscar Arnulfo Romero: at the moment of his victory, he was still officially under refusal by the American State Department for a visa to enter the U.S.

The KGB is heavily involved in Argentina, where the Soviet Union has followed the successful precedent of Cuba and established trade links intended ultimately to make the country economically dependent upon Moscow. Mexico – important like Cuba because of its proximity to the United States – is a priority target of the Soviet intelligence services: in 1971 there were five Mexicans accredited to their legation in Moscow and sixty attached to the Soviet embassy in Mexico.

The military junta of Guatemala, headed by retired General José Efrain Rios Montt, alarmed Washington by the announcement, within weeks after coming to power in a 1982 coup, that he had 'marvellous plans' to improve relations with Cuba and Nicaragua.

President Reagan dispatched from Washington to Havana the multilingual former deputy head of the CIA, General Vernon Walters who speaks seven languages. There is no other leader against whom the United States has considered more assassination plots than Fidel Castro: the approach this time was less violent but more acceptable. Washington offered the economically stretched Castro an alternative to his financial dependence upon Moscow. Unfortunately for Washington, the control of Cuba's intelligence service by the KGB meant that Moscow knew every stage of the American economic approach.

In Russia and East Germany stamps have been issued commemorating the spying activities of Richard Sorge, the German-born GRU officer who ranks as one of the Soviet Union's most successful agents. A Soviet film has also been made, lauding the ability of this man, whose grandfather was secretary to Karl Marx and who has been made a Hero of the Soviet Union.

Stalin ignored Sorge's accurate warning sent from Tokyo in 1941 that Germany was assembling between 170 and 190 divisions to attack Russia. Having made the mistake, he reacted to later information that the Japanese intended moving eastwards, enabling the Red Army to move massive troop concentrations from Siberia to confront Hitler.

Sorge was caught, tried and sentenced to death by the Japanese. On 7 November 1944, he was hanged: the date of his death appears on the Soviet stamp. Long after the romantic rumour persisted that he was not, however, executed but instead swapped in a spy exchange to rise to high executive level within the Russian military service.

It was in Japan, in 1962, that Khrushchev showed the Soviet hypocrisy about its spying activities. He said, 'Espionage is needed by those who prepare for attack, for aggression. The Soviet Union is deeply dedicated to the cause of peace and does not intend to attack anyone. Therefore it has no intention of engaging in espionage.'

It was Khrushchev, in 1953, who brought directly under his and Politburo control the activities of the KGB. Although Khrushchev denounced Stalin, he never criticized Stalin's edict that 'good words are a mask for concealment of bad deeds.'

CHAPTER SEVEN

FEDORA AND THE UNITED NATIONS

His code-name was Fedora. He was Russian. And for more than a decade, apart from a reassignment interruption, he was assessed by America's Federal Bureau of Investigation to be one of the most important and productive spies that they had ever recruited. It was a judgment made not only on the information he provided – just occasionally there were dismissed inconsistencies – but from where he operated. Fedora was a KGB colonel with the cover of a Soviet diplomat attached to the United Nations' towering, green-glassed skyscraper headquarters overlooking New York's East River. The United Nations and its subsidiaries in Geneva and Vienna are diplomatically unique. At the time of writing it is composed of 154 countries. From them, a secretariat of fifteen thousand people, in New York, Vienna, Paris and Geneva, have been chosen not to represent their countries, but to be international civil servants. Upon joining they take an oath – as Fedora did. They cease to be nationals of their country: they are responsible not to one nation but to the United Nations.

The Soviet Union, one of the five permanent members of the Security Council, utterly ignores that principle. Just how flagrantly was disclosed by Arkady Shevchenko, former UN Under Secretary, personal adviser to the Soviet Foreign Minister, Andrei Gromyko, and to Leonid Brezhnev and one-time Ambassador Extraordinary and Plenipotentiary of the U.S.S.R., the country's top diplomatic appointment. Shevchenko, who in 1978 became the highest-ranking Russian ever to defect to the West, said the United Nations was 'the most important base of all Soviet intelligence operations in the world.'

The FBI knew that. They had Fedora. So highly did they regard him that the information he provided was channelled directly into the White House. President Nixon and Henry Kissinger unquestionably believed Fedora's story that a complete set of the Pentagon Papers was delivered to the Soviet embassy on Washington's 16th Street. There was a suggestion to FBI investigators that a minor but nevertheless subsidiary reason why Nixon attempted to cut off the Watergate investigation was his fear that Fedora's identity would be disclosed.

Fedora was a source of wide-ranging information. He even offered details on the Profumo scandal that broke in Britain in 1963. A prostitute, Christine Keeler, shared her bed with the assistant Soviet naval attaché in London, Captain Eugene Ivanov, and the British War Minister, John Profumo. Fedora claimed the Russians succeeded in installing eavesdropping devices in Keeler's bedroom and overheard government secrets being discussed.

One of his most important functions was to guarantee as genuine Yuri Ivanovich Nosenko, who defected in Geneva in 1964. Nosenko said he fled to the West because he was being recalled to Moscow. He also revealed that his rank was that of a lieutenant colonel in the KGB. Fedora said both claims were true. To his delighted debriefers, Nosenko said he was the officer in charge of the KGB file on Lee Harvey Oswald, the assassin of President Kennedy. He said the KGB had never interviewed Oswald during the time he spent in the Soviet Union, nor maintained surveillance on him, nor considered recruiting him as an agent. It was precisely the sort of information that the FBI director, J. Edgar Hoover needed. Hoover wanted nothing to suggest that Oswald was anything but a mentally unstable loner, free from any conspiracy or involvement with a foreign intelligence organization.

The suspicious James Angleton, head of the CIA counterintelligence section, was the first to doubt Nosenko. At his urging, the debriefing by the CIA's Soviet division became an interrogation. Gradually Nosenko confessed to lie after lie: he was jailed, serving part of his sentence in solitary confinement. Surprisingly, the episode did not shake the FBI's confidence in Fedora who continued to supply information from the United Nations and who continued to be believed.

The CIA had a change of heart in 1968. Nosenko was released, appointed a CIA consultant and over the next ten years was paid a total of $500,000 (£208,000) in fees, bonuses and expenses. In 1978 the Agency took the unusual step of issuing a statement in which they called Nosenko 'a well-adjusted American citizen utilized as a consultant by the CIA and making a valuable contribution to our mission.'

The FBI's unshakeable faith in Fedora appeared justified. It was not. In September 1981, the embarrassed Bureau of Investigation conceded that for more than ten years it had been utterly misled by a brilliant Russian intelligence officer fulfilling a classic spy role: peddling disinformation to fool another country's organization and that Fedora had gone home to Russia.

In many ways the career of Fedora closely parallels that of a KGB officer who, for more than a decade, apart from a reassignment interruption, achieved enormous influence and power within the United Nations. His name was Viktor Mechislavovich Lessiovski, who served as special assistant to the Secretary General U Thant and, after his retirement, to Kurt Waldheim. Lessiovski returned to the Soviet Union in June 1981.

Lessiovski's relationship with U Thant was a personal one of friendship. They met in the early 1950s, when U Thant was Minister of Information for Burma and Lessiovski was attached, unknown to the Burmese, as a KGB officer in the Russian embassy in Rangoon. There were house visits and U Thant even called Lessiovski's daughter by a Burmese name.

The friendship was interrupted by Lessiovski's KGB posting to the Thai capital of Bangkok and then by his brief withdrawal to Dzerzhinsky Square, in Moscow. He had already been reappointed, as part of the Soviet delegation to the United Nations, when U Thant became Secretary General in 1961. It is the practise for the Secretary General to compose his personal staff from representatives of the permanent members. Lessiovski became the Soviet appointee. He remained in that position, a KGB man at the very heart of the organization's working, throughout U Thant's period of office and continued to occupy it for the first year of Kurt Waldheim's occupancy.

After Lessiovski's withdrawal from New York, the Russians made a visa application for him to enter Britain. Warned by MI5 of Lessiovski's activities, the Foreign Office refused. In 1977 he was appointed deputy director general of the International Union of Official Travel Organizations, based in Madrid. The Spanish counter-espionage authorities gave their government the same warning that their British counterparts had done in London. The Spanish government protested at Lessiovski's presence and he was withdrawn. Determinedly the Russians proposed him for a second term with the United Nations. He was reappointed special assistant to Kurt Waldheim with a salary of $72,927 (£30,386). Diplomats attached to the UN do not pay tax but instead its equivalent is called a staff assessment. From Lessiovski's salary was deducted staff assessment of $28,007 (£11,698). There is, however, what amounts to a cost-of-living allowance. For Lessiovski this was $15,162 (£6,317) which gave him a salary equivalent of $60,012 (£25,005). There were, of course, diplomatic benefits such as being able to purchase twelve bottles of Scotch for $47 (£19).

In retaliation for the restrictions imposed upon American diplomats in Moscow, the U.S. government limits the travel permitted to Russian diplomats from the Soviet embassy in Washington. If they wish to go beyond a radius of twenty-five miles they must inform the State Department. There are no such hindrances upon Russians attached to the UN. It meant that until his posting ceased in 1981 – the year Fedora stopped being a phoney agent for the FBI – Lessiovski was able to move freely throughout the United States. He took advantage of this, at times lecturing to American universities.

The most recently available statistics show that there were 402 Russians working for the United Nations; most were accompanied by their husbands or wives so that number – the number of potential KGB operatives – can be increased by over half. It does not end there. At the United Nations, as elsewhere, the Soviet Union fully utilizes the services of its satellites. Czechoslovakia has nineteen representatives; East Germany has fifteen; Bulgaria, the dutiful killers of Georgi Markov, has seventeen; Hungary has eleven; Poland has forty; and Cuba has thirty-three. The Ukrainian Republic, hypocritically alleged and supposed to be freely federated with the Soviet Union, has twenty-six. And once again, the majority are accompanied by dependents so these figures, of possible agents, can be almost doubled.

The limited circulation list of the composition of the UN Secretariat in October 1980 shows the influential distribution throughout the United Nations of Russian and satellite countries. Aleksandr Taranenko was assistant chief of protocol. Nikolai Foshine was a director for special political affairs in Kurt Waldheim's office. Vladimir Kartashkin was senior legal officer. Valentin Romanov was the director of the codification division. Mikhail Sytenko, Aleksander Kashirin and Victor Andreev were respectively special assistant and assistant to the under-secretary general in the department of political and security council affairs. The Hungarian, Zoltan Szilagyi, was in charge of the section for co-ordination and political information, with a Russian, Miss Irina Ganina, as an assistant. Sergei Bessabotnov was the political affairs officer in the peace and security studies section. The department responsible for committee and conferences services – giving access to every gathering of each UN division – had Hungarian Pal Csillag as director, Bulgarian Borislav Konstantinov as senior political affairs officer and Russian Guennady Yefimov as political affairs officer, the same rank held by Zdzislaw Matiewicz, a Pole. In the committee services, reports and research section Vyacheslav Shibunyaev was political affairs officer.

In the African division of the United Nations Andrei Ivanovich Petrenko was the political affairs officer. A Ukrainian, Vladimir Fourkalo, was an assistant. Herman Zhilenkov was the economic affairs officer in the mineral resources unit, the same position held by fellow Russian Feliks Ovseenko in the energy resources unit.

A Czech, Karol Kromery, was senior economic affairs officer in the fiscal and financial branch. Yuri Chubarov, a Russian, was the economic affairs officer. A Ukrainian, Vadim Sinchenko, was one of two programmers in the computer systems development and programming section. Vladimir Shevchenko was a Russian statistician in the international trade classification and analysis section.

Of vital importance to a world with a diminishing oil supply are natural resources and energy. A Russian, Anatoli Belov, was an economic affairs officer in the mineral section; his fellow countryman, Aleksandr Drago, had the same title in the department where the maps are drawn, showing the location of such resources throughout the world.

Viktor Yeliseyev was director of the external relations unit of the UN Information Department with Mrs Appolinaria Sentiouleva as his senior assistant. In November 1981, a 111-page booklet issued by that department for use by speakers at United Nations Day celebrations was withdrawn after it was discovered there was no reference to the Soviet invasion of Afghanistan or of the Russian-backed Vietnamese invasion of Cambodia. Sixty thousand copies of the pamphlet had been printed in English. There were more in French and Spanish.

Through the United Nations – in New York, Paris, Vienna or Geneva – pass a constant procession of men and women either on temporary secondment from the governments of their countries or destined, at the end of their period as international civil servants, to return home to become influential members of their administrations. The Soviet Union is vitally interested in every one of them.

In Moscow there is the most detailed and minutely documented record system that exists anywhere in the world. It is called the Central Index. Before the evolution of the computer, the meticulously kept index was housed and maintained in steel-doored rooms and occupied eight floors of an enormous building at Machovaya Ulitza and Vosdvishenka. It has existed since 1918 – recording every conceivable biographical detail about all Russians and any foreigner who might be remotely useful to the security services. In it, until he became Secretary General of the Communist Party and had the file removed, were listed the eighteen aliases (Joseph Besoshvili, Besov, Chizhikov, Ivanov, A. Ivanovich, David, K. Kato, Koba, G. Nizheradze, Ryaboy Soselo, Soso, Oranness, Vartanovich, Totomyans, Vassilyi, Vassilyev, Stalin, J. V. Stalin) of the man whom the world knows as Stalin but whose real name was Joseph Vissarionovich Dzhugashvili. In conversation Lenin only ever referred to him by his revolutionary pseudonym Koba. So comprehensive is the file record that Beria once boasted, 'One would hardly believe how small the great men are in bed or what they are prepared to tell their women.'

The Central Index contains the records of the tens of thousands of UN diplomats and officials who have worked or who are working for it. In the UN in New York, the Russian Nikolai Petrov was, in the last staff list available, the public administration officer in the department responsible for personnel administration. In Geneva, fellow countryman Gely Dneprovsky was chief of the UN personnel services, with Boris Shchuchkin as his assistant.

After Ilya Grigorevich Dzhirkvelov defected from his appointment as press officer to the Geneva-based World Health Organization in April 1980, he named Dneprovsky as a KGB agent. Dzhirkvelov said, 'When you are head of personnel you can look at any file and study a man – his background, his upbringing, his career and his interests. You can discuss his attitudes and actions privately with other heads of departments. You have everything available on your desk which a normal intelligence agent might take many, many months to assemble. It provides a guide to the sort of people who may be possible recruits for Soviet intelligence. It was a brilliant coup for the Soviet Union to secure that position and get one of their top men in as head of personnel.'

Dzhirkvelov claimed that when Kurt Waldheim, on a visit to Geneva, was asked whether Dneprovsky could be a KGB agent, the Austrian-born Secretary General said, 'I don't know. I have no evidence.'

From the refusal of Britain and Spain to accept him there was certainly evidence of Viktor Lessiovski's activities before he resumed his function as Waldheim's special assistant.

In addition to Dneprovsky being the head of personnel in Geneva, the Bulgarian Tzvetan Rachkov was personnel officer in the personnel administration office. Deputy chief of the editorial and documents control section was Valeri Tkatchouk, a Russian. Two Russians, Miss Zinaida Kouzmina and Miss Valentina Serikova, were editors in the section responsible for editing official records. A Cuban, José Cambray, was another editor.

The United Nation's division of human rights is located in Geneva. The Soviet Union is a signatory to the Helsinki agreement, a charter it ignores with the cynicism with which it disregards the UN principle governing the allegiance of Russians working for it. But it is intensely nervous of any criticism of oppression within Russia, always anxious to minimize or deflect the slightest accusation. Within the Geneva division, the Russians are well placed. According to the 1980 listing, Ukrainian Guennadi Lebakine held the title of human rights officer in the research and study unit. A Russian, Yuri Rechetov, was head of the section responsible for preventing discrimination. Boris Pissarev, another Russian, headed the advisory services and publications section and Bulgarian Theodore Dimitrov was in charge of the office acquiring documentation. A Russian, Evgueni Kisselev, was an information officer in the information service, the same role held by another Russian, Mrs Natalyia Berejnaia, in the public relations and documentation unit.

The Warsaw Pact confronts the West in Europe, making Europe strategically vitally important to the Soviet Union. Back in New York there is a secretariat responsible for the Economic Commission for Europe. Russia, or its satellite countries, has obtained thirty-two appointments, gaining positions in every important department.

The Soviet Union was an unenthusiastic founder of the United Nations. From its inception in 1945, Russia viewed the organization not from what it could contribute, but from what it could obtain. The initial advantages were that it obtained a Security Council veto, with which it could effectively bloc any international move the organization attempted to make but with which it did not agree. From the United Nations it could hopefully influence uncommitted countries. And the UN accorded recognition of the Soviet Union as one of the Big Three.

The early years of the UN's existence reflected the Soviet disinterest and obstructiveness: during Stalin's time, the United Nations was barely referred to in any Soviet publication and the improvement was only gradual under Khrushchev. Soviet walk-outs became a wearisome feature of UN debates, enlivened only occasionally by incidents such as Khrushchev hammering with his shoe for attention in 1960.

Exasperated by the shifting attitudes and contradictions of the Soviet Union towards the United Nations, the then British Prime Minister, Harold Macmillan, wrote on 19 July 1960 to Khrushchev. 'I simply do not understand,' complained the British Prime Minister, 'what your purpose is today.'

Twenty-two years later, the question has been answered by a man who had been a confidant of the Politburo of the Soviet Union. Arkady Shevchenko went further than describing the organization as the most important spying base of the Soviet Union. He said, 'Soviet intelligence officers have become the Trojan Horse behind the walls of the UN.'

CHAPTER EIGHT

DISINFORMATION, THE PRIMARY AIM

There was no intention that the secret briefing would ever become public, so the original chief of the KGB's most important section defined its function with surprising honesty. The late General Ivan Ivanovich Agayants said, 'We must constantly encourage Western journalists to write precisely the opposite of our real intentions and anyone who writes or speaks about our real intentions accurately or impartially in the Western sense of these words must quickly be dismissed and ridiculed as someone of the Right or a fascist, someone who wants to bring back McCarthyism.' This is called disinformation.

So vital do the Politburo consider disinformation that in March 1978 they formed an entirely new KGB division, the International Information Department. The director is Leonid Zamyatin, a former head of Tass and protegé and friend of Leonid Brezhnev. That friendship, however, proved Zamyatin's undoing: within three months of becoming the Soviet leader Andropov, wanting to use the International Information Department of the KGB to spearhead his peace campaign and unhappy at its leader's track record, removed Zamyatin from his controlling position. The KGB's previous disinformation section – Department A of the First Chief Directorate – remains in existence and it, too, has been elevated in importance, being upgraded in the early 1970s from department to service status.

An American intelligence analyst judges the formation of the International Information Department as 'a direct result of the Central Committee decision to reorganize the entire foreign propaganda apparatus, improve its effectiveness and open a new propaganda offensive against the West. Its creation signalled the top Soviet leadership's intention to place even greater emphasis on the role of propaganda in foreign policy.' The new function of the upgraded Service A is to plan, co-ordinate and support operations in support of propaganda and covert action.

In the early 1970s Russia reduced its propaganda, considering *détente* to be moving in its favour. The policy was revalued after the slowing-up of arms limitation talks, the reaction to the Soviet presence in Angola and more recently in Afghanistan. Western intelligence give 1976 as the year when the KGB were told by the Politburo to increase massively the propaganda and disinformation to the West.

The KGB regarded the 1980 Olympic Games in Moscow as an unrivalled opportunity for disinformation, despite the setback of the American-led boycott in protest at the invasion of Afghanistan. The Russian Olympic Committee was packed with KGB officers. Vladimir Popov, decorated by Stalin for partisan work behind the Nazi lines, was vice-chairman. A. A. Gresko, one of the 105 diplomats expelled from London in 1971 for spying, was also a member. So, too, was a man whose name was given as S. Nikitin. His real name was Anatoli Gorsky; sometimes he used another alias, Anatoli Gromov. It was Gorsky who from 1936 to 1944 controlled, from the Russian embassy in London, Kim Philby, Donald Maclean, Guy Burgess and Anthony Blunt. Before his appointment to the Olympic Committee Gorsky was frequently introduced to visiting Western history students as Professor Nikitin, of the Institute of History.

John McMahon, deputy director of the CIA, warned American politicians in 1980 when he was deputy director for Operations, 'There is a tendency sometimes in the West to play down the significance of foreign propaganda and to cast doubts on the efficacy of covert action as instruments of foreign policy. Soviet leaders, however, do not share such beliefs. They regard propaganda and covert action as auxiliary instruments in the conduct of their foreign policy by conventional diplomatic, military and economic means.'

The KGB describe covert action as *aktivnye meropriyatiya*: a literal translation is 'active measures'. Within the International Information Department and Service A those active measures include written or oral disinformation, forgery, the creation of false rumour, manipulation and control of foreign media, the manipulation of political action in foreign countries, the use of agents of influence, the use of clandestine radio stations, use and manipulation of foreign communist parties and international front groups, support for internal revolutionary and terrorist groups and if possible political blackmail.

The CIA are aware that Russia defines the United States as its main enemy and at its headquarters at Langley, Virginia, they have created an assessment of the Politburo's aims. They are, according to CIA analysts, to influence both world and American public opinion against U.S. military and political programmes considered threatening to the Soviet Union; to show the U.S. as an aggressive colonial and imperialistic power; to isolate the U.S. from its allies and friends; to discredit those who co-operate with the U.S. and to demonstrate that the policies and goals of the U.S. are against the interests of underdeveloped or Third World countries.

The most successful disinformation exercise in recent years has been the forgery of an American army field manual. There is a genuine manual FM 30–31B.

There is also the Russian copy, perfect in its use of correct paper, printing, military jargon and phraseology. Its one mistake is the Top Secret designation, which is too high a classification. It purports to be operational guidance to U.S. military security services in influencing the internal affairs of friendly countries where U.S. armed forces are based and which have internal security, terrorist or subversive problems. It recommends the U.S. services infiltrate the Left organizations and turn them to American advantage, to the detriment of the host government.

So cleverly is it forged – even to the re-creation of the signature of General William Westmoreland – that it has been accepted as a genuine indication of American interference in foreign governments by newspapers and publications in more than twenty countries.

The Russian version of FM 30–31B first appeared in a Turkish newspaper, *Baris*, in the autumn of 1975. A year later, a copy was found pinned to a noticeboard in the Philippine embassy in the Thai capital of Bangkok. In 1978 its publication in Spain can be directly traced to the Soviet and Cuban intelligence services. A copy of the manual was made available by Boris Grigoriyevich Karpov, the KGB rezident at the Soviet embassy in Madrid. He gave it to a known member of the Communist Party, Fernando Gonzalez, who wrote an article 'disclosing' its secrets. This article was distributed to *El Triunfo*, in which it was published, and other Spanish publications by Luis Gonzalez Verdecia, a diplomat attached to the Cuban embassy in Madrid. Verdecia is a member of Cuba's Direccion General de Inteligencia.

After the Italian Christian Democrat leader, Aldo Moro, was assassinated by the Red Brigade terrorists in 1978, articles appeared in several Italian newspapers citing the manual as evidence that the CIA was involved. The claim was widely believed in Italy by a section of the public who regards the Red Brigade as a Fascist, right-wing organization rather than one of the Marxist left.

So concerned are the U.S. government and the CIA about forgeries like this, and others, that officials have been sent from Washington and diplomats instructed at various embassies to assure host governments of American innocence. The CIA try to react within twenty-four hours of recognizing a forgery.

The Middle East has been a particular target of such forgeries. One, leaked to Arab and Western newspapers, was supposed to be advice from the U.S. ambassador to Cairo, Herman F. Eilts, to the then CIA Director Admiral Stansfield Turner if the late President Anwar Sadat refused to advance U.S. interests. The bogus message said, 'We must repudiate him and get rid of him without hesitation.'

The same communication indicated CIA infiltration and control of the Palestine Liberation Organization. Eilts was supposed to have suggested a policy shift of PLO leaders towards Israel. The letter said, 'I know you possess the necessary capability and resources in this regard.'

During the American administration of President Jimmy Carter, the Russians fabricated statements alleged to have come from the vice-president, Walter Mondale, claiming that Israel's leader Menachem Begin, who suffers from a heart condition, was terminally ill and that Sadat was losing control of Egypt.

Notes supposed to have been taken by an aide of the U.S. Secretary of State, Cyrus Vance, were mailed to the Egyptian embassy in Rome, again with the purported signature of

Ambassador Eilts. In these notes Sadat, Jordan's King Hussein, Syria's President Assad and the Saudi Arabian and Kuwaiti leadership were discussed and dismissed contemptuously.

In the autumn of 1976 a genuine American State Department instruction to U.S. embassies in Western Europe to collect publicly available economic, commercial and financial information was altered so that it indicated orders to collect facts that could be used to bribe European officials and create plans of covert measures to hinder or eliminate foreign trade competition.

In mid-1978 the Russians issued a bogus letter written on official NATO stationery but bearing the forged signature of Joseph Luns. The letter informed the U.S. ambassador to NATO that the Belgian Defence Ministry had compiled a list of journalists opposed to the deployment in Europe of the neutron bomb. The inference was that these journalists were to be penalized for their 'negative' reporting.

A CIA concern about these forgeries is that for them to be of such a high quality, the KGB must have examples of genuine classified material, with access to the correct paper, ink and printing machines. And it is unaware of what – or where – that source is.

One of the best-known exponents of Soviet disinformation is Vitali Yevgennevich Lui, who writes for Western publications under the fittingly westernized name of Victor Louis. His articles have appeared in *The New York Times* and *The Washington Post*. When it had the largest circulation of any evening newspaper in the world, the now defunct London *Evening News* was the natural outlet and Louis wrote for it with the Russians actually content for the West to know he was an official source! Frequently – satisfied his stories would be recognized and accepted as official – policy was planted and acted upon. A story in the *Evening News* – picked up and repeated in Australia, where the Communist Party has links as strong with Peking as it has with Moscow – that the Russians did not wish to exacerbate a confrontation with the Chinese on their border at the Ussari River was sufficient for a relieved China to de-escalate their apparent belligerence. Louis was used, unsuccessfully, in a KGB effort to discredit the memoirs of Svetlana Stalin at a politically awkward time.

He is known, and surprisingly accepted, in high places. Hubert Humphrey was visited by Louis when Humphrey was vice-president of the United States in 1966. Henry Kissinger permitted an interview in 1971. Like Leonid Brezhnev, Louis delights in expensive foreign cars. His favourite car is a Mercedes – Brezhnev has one too. Louis also likes westernized electronic gadgetry. Some years ago a telephone was put on to the American market whose summons was not a bell but a light that went on and off in the handpiece. Louis was proud of it in his elaborate Moscow apartment. It did not work, of course. Russian telephone technology was not geared for such an invention. Perhaps – for a Soviet disinformation expert – a telephone that is impossible to use is considered an advantage.

With disinformation, as with every other espionage activity, the Soviet Union heavily utilizes its satellite services. The defection and subsequent information provided by Ladislav Bittman disclosed the extent of that use. Bittman was head of the disinformation department – designated number 8 of the Czech intelligence service.

He told U.S. investigating senators, 'Satellite countries operate huge intelligence apparatuses that significantly contribute to the spreading of Soviet influence around the world.' And added that from their inception after World War II every communist-bloc intelligence service operated under Russian control. Each department, disinformation included, had its own Soviet adviser, 'a man who was a specialist in intelligence service problems and who saw every report: who knew the identity of every agent: who received everything that the service produced – they were the managers.'

It was the disinformation service of Czech intelligence – on KGB orders – that orchestrated the campaign against Senator Barry Goldwater when he ran for the presidency of America in 1964. Bittman recounts, 'Goldwater was considered a very dangerous opponent, a very strong adversary, and the Soviets were thinking about how to influence the election process.'

The result was a booklet. 'In the text,' said Bittman, 'there were some genuine statements by Goldwater and then some statements manufactured indicating his racism. Mainly it was supposed racist policies or whatever and this was then distributed to the U.S. and abroad. It was sent to many journalists and politicians in developing countries. I think the result was much more successful in developing countries than in the U.S.'

Every year officers within the disinformation departments of the communist countries have to forward to Dzerzhinsky Square suggestions for an anti-West campaign. Bittman claims one of his ideas actually resulted in the West German government extending the statute of limitations under which Nazi war criminals could be tried.

On the West German–Czech border are two lakes. One is Devil's Lake and the other is Black Lake. Since World War II there has always been the rumour that fleeing Nazis at the end of the war used the lakes, and also Lake Toplitz in Austria, to sink incriminating records. While still working with Czech intelligence Bittman learned that Czech television was making a film using the lakes as a location. What followed was Bittman's idea, judged by Moscow to be unquestionably one of the best ever submitted by a disinformation expert. At night Bittman and other STB officers sank in the lake four boxes specially treated to indicate long submersion. They then directed the film crew divers to where they were. The triumphant surfacing of the boxes was then filmed. Then the Czech Foreign Minister, Lubomir Strougal, announced at a press conference that an enormous number of Nazi documents, including a list of Nazi agents in Eastern Europe, had been raised from the lakes.

The announcement was devastating. The West German intelligence organization after the war picked up and formed networks from Nazi agents; the Czech claim effectively meant that the identity of every agent was exposed.

To get the limitations statute extended, Strougal offered 'thousands of documents about Nazi war crimes.' To maintain the bluff, the KGB had to supply captured documents from Moscow because those in the Czech archives were insufficient. By careful and controlled leaking to the European press, the Czechs and the KGB managed to maintain the 'boxes from the lake' disinformation for a full two years before the campaign was finally halted. It was not until several years afterwards that Western – and German – intelligence realized how they had been duped.

There were many former Nazis serving in the West German government who lived throughout that time daily fearing exposure. Some resigned. It was a classic disinformation operation. Appropriately it was code-named Neptune.

A KGB training manual smuggled to the West says in part, 'Strategic disinformation assists in the execution of state tasks and is directed at misleading the enemy concerning the basic questions of State policy, the military and economic status and the scientific and technical achievements of the Soviet Union.'

No country and no intelligence service performs that task better than the Soviet Union's KGB.

CHAPTER NINE

THE TRADECRAFT OF SPYING

From 1945, when Igor Gouzenko fled to asylum in Canada with a mass of Soviet espionage documentation, Western intelligence has gained intriguing insights into the flowery descriptions with which the Russians wrap their spying activities.

Code-names, of course, are an obvious precaution for cell protection: but even within the cells people are referred to by these names, in the hope that partial detection will not lead to the identification of all. Gouzenko, who was a cipher clerk, had the not-original code-name of Klark. The commercial counsellor showed more originality; his cover was the Economist. The GRU director of Gouzenko's Canadian cell was called Colonel Zabotin with a code-name of Grant and the interpreter Runy.

It was through this cell that the Russians obtained from Alan Nunn May – his code-name was Alek – the secrets of the atomic bomb experiments being carried out at Chalk River, Ontario, together with a sample of Uranium 235.

Nunn May was a secret communist before he left Britain for Canada to take part in atomic research. He had been working for the Russians for at least two years. May provided information of incalculable value to Moscow, with corresponding damage to the West. He returned to England from Canada at the end of 1945 and the cables that passed between Grant and the headquarters in Moscow show the classic Soviet tradecraft and at the same time the obstructive refusal of the Centre in Moscow to permit their agents on the spot to operate with any degree of independence.

The cables reprinted here are to arrange continuous contact with May upon his return to London and passed between an unknown director at the headquarters in Moscow and Grant from the sealed cipher room in the Soviet embassy in Ottawa.

From Moscow   30.7.45.
To Grant
Reference No. 218
(22.7.45)

Work out and telegraph arrangements for the meeting
and password of Alek with our man in London.

From Ottawa   31.7.45
Grant
To the Director

We have worked out the conditions of a meeting with
Alek in London. Alek will work in King's College, Strand.
It will be possible to find him there through the telephone
book.

Meetings: October 7.17.27 on the street in front of the
British Museum. The time, eleven o'clock in the evening.
Identification signal: a newspaper under the left arm.
Password: 'Best regards to Mikel'.

He [Nunn May] cannot remain in Canada. At the
beginning of September he must fly to London. Before his
departure he will go to the Uranium Plant in the Petawawa
district where he will be for about two weeks. He promised,
if possible, to meet us before his departure. He said that he
must come next year for a month to Canada. We handed
over 500 dollars to him. Grant.

To Grant   22.8.45
Reference No. 244

The arrangements worked out for the meeting are not
satisfactory. I am informing you of new ones.

1. Place:

In front of the British Museum in London, on Great
Russell Street, at the opposite side of the Street, about
Museum Street, from the side of Tottenham Court Road,
repeat Tottenham Court Road. Alek walks from Tottenham Court Road, the contact man from the opposite
side – Southampton Row.

2. Time:

As indicated by you, however, it would be more
expedient to carry out the meeting at 20 o'clock if it should

be convenient to Alek, as at 23 o'clock it is too dark. As for the time, agree about it with Alek and communicate the decision to me. In case the meeting should not take place in October, the time and day will be repeated in the following months.

3. Identification signs:

Alek will have under his left arm the newspaper, *The Times*, the contact man will have in his left hand the magazine, *Picture Post*.

4. The password:

The contact man: 'What is the shortest way to the Strand?'

Alek: 'Well, come along, I am going that way.'

In the beginning of the business conversation Alek says 'Best regards from Mikel.'

Report on transmitting the conditions to Alek 18.8. Director. 22.8.45.

There was no indication at Nunn May's subsequent trial – when he was sentenced to ten years in jail – whether the meeting took place.

Counter-espionage raids in Sweden in 1951 and 1952 and again in 1952 in Paris, Lyon and Toulon disclosed the Russian insistence upon written material, but embarrassingly for Moscow, that material remained to incriminate their agents. This resulted in greater use by the Centre of microdot and micro-photography. During his evidence to the Australian Royal Commission, Petrov said communications between himself and Moscow had been carried on undeveloped film protected by lightproof paper. If opened in a search, the film immediately 'fogged', destroying anything that might have been incriminating. Agents' names, code-names and addresses were recorded on inflammable film, which could be destroyed within seconds if discovery was feared. The *resident* director had to send Moscow a certificate guaranteeing that any order to destroy a document had actually been carried out. Unfortunately for the Centre, in Canada it was Igor Gouzenko to whom the destruction was entrusted by Colonel Zabotin.

Tradecraft instruction to another atom spy, Dr Klaus Fuchs, was that he should carry a tennis ball and his contact,

Harry Gold, gloves and a book. David Greenglass was part of this same American cell. At their first meeting, Gold carried a torn packet of jelly powder for identification. The missing half matched that carried by Greenglass's wife. The password was, 'I come from Julius.'

One of the most incredibly successful spy rings during World War II was the Red Orchestra, which provided Moscow with astonishing details from within the heart of Hitler's war cabinet. An Englishman, Alexander Foote, was part of it. After the war he was withdrawn to Russia for further instruction and then infiltrated back into a divided Berlin. He lived at Wisbyerstrasse 41, Pankov. And he had a tradecraft arrangement for emergency contact with the Centre.

Foote describes it, 'In case the Centre wished to contact me, I was to go on the last Sunday in every month to the Prenzlauer Station, carrying a leather belt in one hand and my hat in the other. If the Centre wished to contact me, someone would come up to me and say *Wann fährt der letzte Zug ab?* [When does the last train go?] My reply was *Seit Morgen um 22 uhr.* [Since tomorrow at 10 p.m.]. If, on the other hand, I wanted to contact the Centre, all I had to do was to put a notice on a certain public notice board in Berlin reading *Such Kinderfahrrad. A Kleber, Muristrasse 12, Berlin/Gruenau.* [Wanted, a child's bicycle] and the next day an agent of the Centre would come to the place of conspiracy at the Prenzlauer Station. He would come straight up and say that he had seen an advertisement, for I would be known to him by sight as a result of my monthly visits.'

In 1961 the KGB recruited from the British Ministry of Defence a spy named Frank Bossard. His instructions were to listen on specified nights to Radio Moscow and his orders were carried in a code worked out on five tunes – 'Song of the Volga Boatmen', 'Swan Lake', 'Moscow Nights', 'The Sabre Dance' and 'Kalinka'.

In his exhaustively researched book – *KGB: – The Secret Work of Soviet Secret Agents* – John Barron records the elaborate tradecraft that had to be followed by Kaarlo Tuomi, a KGB illegal detected and then turned as a double by America's FBI. It started from the moment Tuomi stepped off the Kirov train at Moscow's Yaroslavsky station for his training.

A man said, 'Good morning. Tell me, how is your Uncle Yefim?'

Tuomi obediently replied, 'I'm sorry to say he just passed away.'

Satisfied, the contact said, 'That's too bad. Come with me please.'

Installed as an illegal in the United States, Tuomi was given 'post boxes' through which to communicate with the Centre – with messages left in magnetized containers – beneath a railway bridge in the New York borough of Queens, by a lamp-post on the northeast corner of St Michael's Cemetery, also in Queens, beneath an underground bridge at the Bronx and below a bush near McLean and Van Cortlandt Avenues, in Yonkers. Russia's spy centre in America, the United Nations, was the contact point he had to alert by an innocuous postcard that messages were ready for collection. Later the instructions became more detailed. He had to walk a certain route every Saturday morning, looking for dropped orange peel. If there was some in the road, it meant he had to go to one of his post boxes to receive a message. Acknowledgment was again by card to the UN.

After Tuomi's detection and turning by the FBI, the Bureau surrendered some genuine secrets and the Centre was impressed. So much so that the KGB decided Tuomi should have a meeting with another Russian agent in America, something he had been told would never happen. The indication of a meeting came in a way he had been trained to recognize – the delivery in the ordinary mail of advertisements with the lower left-hand corner folded, to indicate that the reverse sides contained encoded instructions.

Deciphered, the message from Moscow read, 'We announce the conditions of a meeting. Time: Sunday, 23 September 0900 hours. Place: the bank of the river Hudson opposite the Greystone railway station in Westchester County. With fishing rods, a rose-coloured plastic pail and a fishing licence, drive to the northern part of the town of Yonkers. Then drive along Warburton Avenue to Greystone station and park your car in the parking lot. Cross the pedestrian bridge to the river and then walk along the bank to the telephone pole with the figure 429. Near this pole you should be fishing. Parole (recognition signal) "Excuse me, I think we met at the Yonkers Yacht Club last year." You must answer "No, sir, I left that club in 1960." Legend of contact: you met your representative while fishing. Report your readiness for the meeting by sending a religious postcard to our United Nations mission. Sign the card R. Sands. If you do not understand the conditions of the meeting, sign the card D. C. Kott.'

The fellow fisherman on the banks of the Hudson was Aleksei Ivanovich Galkin, who had instructed him in Moscow. Galkin's mission was to entrust three other Soviet agents to Tuomi's control. For almost a year Tuomi remained a double, before defecting to America. He was then provided with a new identity by the FBI.

In April 1982, FBI agents seized fifty-year-old Hungarian Otto Attila Gilbert in the act of receiving classified documents near a Confederate War Memorial in Augusta, Georgia. Since 1977 Hungarian military intelligence, of which Gilbert was a member, had been cultivating the Hungarian-born U.S. Army Warrant officer Janos Szmolka, not knowing that from the moment of their first approach Szmolka had warned U.S. counter-espionage agents.

The code for the Augusta meeting was for Gilbert to approach Szmolka and say, 'Where is the Peachtree Plaza Hotel? I am from out of town.' Szmolka's identification was to carry a multicoloured camera strap over his right shoulder and an issue of the *Augusta Herald* in his right hand.

To indicate that he had the material the Hungarian wanted – and to trap their agent – Szmolka had written to a maildrop in Paris that he had obtained '1964 Kennedy half dollars'. To indicate it was army material, Szmolka said the dollars were in 'mint condition'. In return, he received a Vienna-postmarked letter telling him 'Isobelle is getting married.' The date of the meeting between Szmolka and Gilbert, 27 April, was described as the 'wedding date'.

The KGB's use of technological tradecraft emerged in 1978 with the arrest in Teheran of the army's deputy chief of logistics, General Mogharebi, and an Education Ministry official, Ali Naghi Rabbani. Instructions from the Centre came by radio signals, beamed from an orbiting satellite and picked up on a receiving set which appeared to be a pocket calculator. Rabbini, who was the cut-out, simply had to reverse the calculator and the figures became letters from which he could read his orders.

Mogharebi recorded the information he wished to communicate on a miniaturized tape recorder. His KGB contact at no time had to approach him. He merely parked near Mogharebi's villa according to a pre-arranged schedule, with a receiving set. Both were equipped for speeded transmission; twenty minutes of conversation or detailed information could be relayed between one and the other in twenty seconds.

I have referred earlier to the thirteen Russians expelled from Ottawa in 1978. The tradecraft developed for that operation involved a Mountie, whom the Centre wrongly imagined was working for them, making contact by sticking tape on a pillar in an Ottawa shopping area. From the Centre came the explicit instructions for the use of the tape. 'Vertical position of the tape – the operation takes place in Montreal. Horizontal position – operation takes place in Ottawa. Yellow colour – call for the regular meeting. Black colour – call for an instant meeting.'

Phoney information was passed on to the Russians in hollowed-out sticks and in an apparently discarded packet of Marlboro cigarettes. Contact was strictly regimented. The man whom the KGB believed to be an agent had to park and lift the bonnet of his car, having already left a copy of *McLean*'s magazine on the rear shelf, where it would be visible through the window. He then had to wait for a man to come up and ask, 'Can you show me the way to Pink Lake?'

Orange peel seems a favourite identification signal in Moscow. As with Tuomi in New York, the Canadians were instructed to drop peel at a pre-arranged spot to show that a message had been secreted in an earlier thrown-away Coca-Cola can. As the KGB has learned to its embarrassed cost orange peel, like that of the banana, is very easy to slip up on.

CHAPTER TEN

TO DEFECT IS TO DIE

Karel Zizka talked about it with his wife until there was nothing further left to say, because he and Vera always came up against the same obstacle. Karel could not defect from the UN mission in New York while their two children remained hostage in Prague.

Christmas comes early in New York. By October the advertisements were appearing in the newspapers, and the shop windows along Fifth Avenue were decorated. It was then that Vera got her idea. Karel thought it would work.

The following day he made the formal application, both to the Czech consulate at the UN, where he was a code clerk, and to Prague, for his children to be allowed to join their parents for Christmas in New York. This gave the KGB the date when Karel intended to flee. It is uncertain how the Russians discovered his intention to defect. The likeliest explanation is that the apartment in which the Zizkas lived was bugged; it was an official residence, part of the Czech diplomatic housing complex.

The message to Colonel Miloslav Vejvoda came direct from Moscow's Centre. There had to be positive confirmation. Then the Zizkas were to be deported back to Prague immediately. If there was any difficulty, then the matter had to be resolved another way.

Vejvoda, whose alias was Bartos, was a long-standing loyal agent of the Czech secret police, the Statni Tajna Bezpecnost. He had served for two terms at the Czech embassy in Washington, had been a deputy administrator for Foreign Affairs and Czech ambassador to the Geneva Disarmament Commission. At the time Karel and Vera Zizka planned to defect, he was serving on the Czech UN delegation.

On 18 October 1962, Zizka was on night duty. It was then that Colonel Vejvoda visited Vera. He was not alone; an unidentified KGB man accompanied him. The Russian was attached to the Executive Action Department, the killer section, of the First Chief Directorate of the KGB.

Karel Zizka's duty did not end until 9 a.m. but he broke the rules, returning home two hours early. Vejvoda and the Russian were surprised, not ready for him. No more so than Karel Zizka was ready for what confronted him as he stood in the doorway.

Medical examination later showed that Vera Zizka had been tortured by having her face slashed and slowly stripped by a razor. Meat tenderisor had been poured into the wounds. By the time her husband arrived home, Vera Zizka's agony was over; she had been shot in the head.

Karel Zizka's reaction was panicked but immediate. Before he could be prevented, he turned and ran. Outside the apartment he managed to reach his car and drove hysterically off through the streets of New York, so hysterically that a police chase began almost at once. It did not last long. Zizka crashed the car near a bridge. Before the pursuing policemen reached him, he shot himself.

The Czechs demanded the return, under diplomatic immunity, of Karel Zizka's body but the American authorities refused, carrying out a post-mortem examination first. The Czechs, to support their account of what happened, allowed police and investigators from the district attorney's office to visit the Zizka apartment, even though it was official diplomatic territory. On the tablecloth was the alleged suicide note. It said: 'I have gone mad. I killed my wife. Goodbye.'

The Americans had no difficulty reading it. The supposedly insane Karel Zizka – after torturing and then murdering his wife – had had the forethought to write it in English. The Americans requested permission to carry out an autopsy on the body of Vera Zizka. It was refused. It would, of course, have disclosed a different calibre of bullet from that with which Karel Zizka killed himself.

The Zizka children never saw Christmas in New York. Instead they went to a funeral in Prague.

A person who defects from the Soviet Union or any of its satellites is a traitor and although not automatic the sentence is almost invariably death. Each year the KGB produces, for circulation to all their legal *rezidents* abroad and for their internal departments, a 460-page book. It is stamped *sovershenno sekretnoe* – top secret – and contains biographies and details of approximately 1,130 people on the KGB-wanted list.

Defecting ballet star Rudolf Nureyev is one of those listed. His entry reads, 'While on tour in France on June 16, 1961, he betrayed his country. In 1962 the Leningrad City court sentenced him to seven years deprivation of freedom. He lives in London.'

Vladimir Kostov lives in Paris. Kostov was a major figure in Bulgaria, head of the Paris bureau of the state radio and a political expert who had worked in Russia, the Middle East and Europe. In June 1977, he defected with his wife Natalya: three months later, in London, Georgi Markov received a telephone call from his brother Nikola in Italy. Nikola said the Bulgarians were blaming Markov for Kostov's defection.

Three weeks before Georgi Markov was stabbed walking across Waterloo Bridge, Kostov emerged from the Paris Metro near the Arc de Triomphe. He heard what he later described as a muffled crack, like an airgun report. And at once felt a sting in his back.

At a clinic in Nanterre minute metal fragments – identical to the pellet discovered in Markov's body – were extracted from his back. The pellet hardly penetrated Kostov: it had been blocked by the thick cardigan he was wearing. He survived. The pellet taken from Kostov was sent to London, for forensic comparison with that which killed Markov. Kostov worked with police and security artists, creating a Photofit picture of the man he had seen close to him at the Arc de Triomphe.

The day after Markov was attacked a 45-year-old Bulgarian doctor, a defector like Kostov and Markov, vanished from a hospital at which he worked in Weissenburg, about 100 miles from Munich. The doctor later reappeared. Detectives from Britain and France, with Kostov's Photofit picture, interviewed the man, who denied any part or knowledge of the attacks upon either of his fellow countrymen. Kostov attended an identity parade at which the Bulgarian doctor was arraigned but failed to identify him.

Police were particularly interested in the doctor because forensic scientists in Britain said that although the pellet that killed Markov could have come from the tip of an umbrella it could also have been fired by a surgical gun concealed within the umbrella's folds. The implantation gun is normally used by doctors to inject radioactive gold pellets under the skin for the treatment of skin cancer. Such treatment was practised at Weissenburg.

Kostov sent a wreath to Markov's funeral in Dorset, England. The inscription read, 'In honour of Georgi's cause and sacrifice.'

In 1937 Walter Krivitsky, chief of Soviet military intelligence in Western Europe, defected to America. His book, *I Was Stalin's Agent*, was one of the first indications of the bloodletting that was going on within the Soviet Union, under Stalin's orders. Krivitsky survived for four years. In 1941 he was shot in a Washington hotel. In his book, *My Silent War*, Philby asserts that Krivitsky committed suicide. Philby nominally works for Novosti but his function is predominantly KGB disinformation; knowing that his letters to England are opened, he regularly includes things hoping to confuse British intelligence. Philby has also written postcards, stamped in Cuba, to the novelist, Graham Greene – they were once friends – knowing that they will be published. American intelligence, who believe that Philby has genuinely travelled to Havana and not had them posted for him, consider the effect of their publicity important to the KGB. It makes clear to any undetected agents that eventual flight does not mean a permanent, unmoving domicile in the Soviet Union. But Philby's assertion about Krivitsky, whose defection and revelations about Stalin enraged the Soviet dictator, was a lie. Krivitsky did not commit suicide. He was assassinated by killers from the Executive Action Department of the First Chief Directorate.

Instead of killing his victim – Georgi Sergeevich Okolovich, leader of the Soviet émigré group *Narodnyi Trudovoi Soyuz* – trained assassin Nikolai Khokhlov defected. With him he brought a gold cigarette case which was, in reality, an electric pistol that fired poisoned Dum Dum bullets. For three years Khokhlov spoke publicly and at embarrassing length about the assassination activities of the KGB. Suddenly he became ill. His body swelled, his skin became discoloured and his hair fell out. Medical examination showed that his white blood corpuscles were being destroyed, his bones decaying, his blood turning to plasma and his saliva glands withering. Although there is some scientific uncertainty whether it is technically possible, physicians who managed to save Khokhlov's life decided that he had been poisoned with thallium, a toxic metal, which had first been permeated with atomic radiation.

To defect from Russia is to become its enemy and Stalin issued the dictum which the KGB follows with regard to such people. He said, 'Sleep is sweetest after you have settled an account with your enemy.'

CHAPTER ELEVEN

THE LABOUR CAMPS

The transportation maps of the Soviet Union show the railway line that drops in a southeastern direction from Moscow, to Saransk and then on to Kuybyshev. There is another track, a spur line, jutting northwards from Potma. It runs for about thirty-seven miles, right up to Barashevo. It has stations, such as Lesnoy, Selkos and Lepley, and the attendants wear uniforms, although not like those of the rest of the Russian railway staff. The Potma-Barashevo line does not appear on any official map, either, because officially it does not exist. Since Lavrenti Beria's almost successful bid for power after Stalin's death, the State security service, the KGB, has been separated from the MVD, the Ministry for Internal Affairs. The Potma-Barashevo line is the responsibility of the MVD; in reality, it is a transport system for the KGB to carry prisoners to the thirty-six camps so vast that through the cracks in the moving prison cars they appear as one continuous stretch – camp and then cemetery, cemetery and then camp.

This complex is just one of many, part of the Gulag (acronym for Labour Camp Administration) Archipelago of Aleksandr Solzhenitsyn. There are other complexes, at Sverdlovsk, Chelyabinsk, Magnitogorsk, Perm and Verkhneuralsk in the Urals. In Siberia they exist at Krasnoyarsk, Novosibirsk, Tomsk, Irkutsk, Tayshet and Chita. During the Stalin era, throughout the enormous area of Kolyma – it is four times the size of France – there were over 100 camps, a large proportion of which still remain. In addition to a term of imprisonment, Russian courts frequently imposed terms of exile. The huge region of Kazakhstan is virtually populated by exiled ex-prisoners: 70 per cent of the population of Karaganda originated from labour camps.

Lenin evolved the camps but Stalin perfected their obscene use. It was during Stalin's dictatorial regime that they became an extermination machinery more efficient than that of the

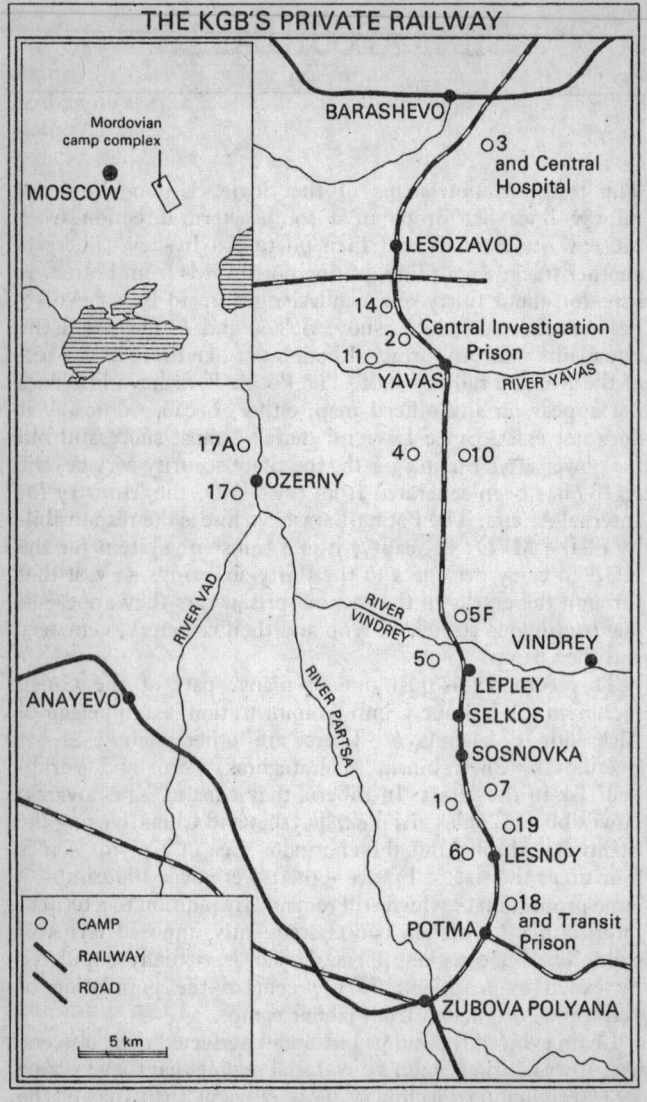

THE KGB'S PRIVATE RAILWAY

BARASHEVO

○3
and Central
Hospital

LESOZAVOD

14○
2○ Central Investigation
11○ Prison
YAVAS   RIVER YAVAS

Mordovian
camp complex

MOSCOW

17A○
17○ OZERNY   4○   ○10

RIVER
VINDREY   ○5F
RIVER VAD   5○   VINDREY
LEPLEY
SELKOS
RIVER PARTSA   SOSNOVKA
ANAYEVO   1○   ○7
○19
6○ LESNOY
○18
POTMA   and Transit
Prison
ZUBOVA POLYANA

○   CAMP
RAILWAY
ROAD

5 km

Third Reich. After World War II there were estimated to be fourteen million people in the Soviet prison system. A conservative calculation of the number who died in camps during Stalin's rule is put at twelve million. I have seen figures double that amount: from the vast size of the prison complex and the length of Stalin's rule I put it higher than twelve million.

Since Stalin the labour-camp system has been reduced; prison population now is estimated at two million. But the harshness endures, both in treatment and conditions. I spoke at length in Moscow to a Briton within hours of his release from the Potma complex, before he had time to embellish his account by reading those of other released prisoners. He talked of a method recounted by prisoners from other camps of obliterating the awfulness of their existence in a few moments of narcotic inebriation by boiling as large a quantity of tea as possible in a minimum amount of water, creating a thick brown liquid. Compared to some, the man, who came from Newcastle and who had been jailed for brawling in Leningrad, fared well. He sold his nylon-quilted jacket to a prison guard and with the money set up a black market within his prison selling tea. The jailed British teacher, Gerald Brooke, was a contemporary.

The man, a seaman, talked too of men driven to such a point of desperation that in order to avoid the gruelling, unremitting work they would mutilate or injure themselves. He had seen a prisoner bribe another to crush his readily offered fingers against a post-end with a hammer. Stories of such mutilations are frequent in accounts from camps throughout the Soviet Union. During the height of the horror under Stalin, there were instances from Kolyma of prisoners severing toes for a few days respite, injecting kerosine under their skins to create an infection and purposely wrapping wet cloths around their feet, to induce frostbite in temperatures that sometimes in the region reach minus 70 degrees.

In conditions colder than anywhere else on earth, issued underwear was handkerchief thin. Quilted jackets and trousers were insufficient to prevent frostbite, even when not purposely induced; the clothes were nearly always soaked from being out in the frozen tundra and were stolen if left in the drying rooms at the entrances to most barracks. Prisoners trying to prevent frostbite wrapped any scrap of cloth around their feet for added protection. The thick, heavy paper from cement bags used during construction work became black market material: it could be wrapped around the body, for extra protection against the cold. Sacking and canvas were used for boots, rather than felt which was introduced later. Soles were made from worn-out car tyres. The boots became waterlogged and at the end of the day it was all but impossible for prisoners to put one foot in front of the other. During his denunciation period of Stalin, Khrushchev allowed the fact to be published in the Soviet Union that work norms had been imposed in the labour camps, for a twelve-hour *basic* minimum working day, which was often extended to sixteen hours. A prisoner achieving his norm was permitted 800 grams of bread. If the norm was unfulfilled, the ration was cut to 500 grams. Food rationing was cut further, as a method of punishment. Three hundred grams meant starvation. Prisoners ate lubrication grease, moss and the carcases of any animals, irrespective of how putrid and rotting the flesh. The recognized minimum calorie intake for someone working a hard, eight-hour day is between 3,100 and 3,900. Even by 1977 the calorie allowance in strict regime camps was only 2,600. Punishment diet was 2,100 and prisoners on strict punishment conditions received 1,300 a day. In Stalin's Kolyma, to combat endemic scurvy caused by vitamin deficiency, prisoners were made to drink water in which pine needles and the leaves of dwarf willow had been brewed. Lice and insect infestation was so great that typhus epidemics occurred.

Political prisoners were housed with common criminals, called *urkas*, who terrorized them, robbing and raping. To survive in women's camps the inmates frequently turned to prostitution – in his book *Kolyma* Robert Conquest estimates that at its height, the prison complex of that vast region housed 25,000 women. A camp at Elgen was the delegated place for women to give birth to any child resulting from rape or prostitution or any association with male prisoners. A mother could stay with her child for a week after its birth and was off work for a month. She was not allowed into the children's rooms, but was permitted to nurse her child in a visiting area. After nine months the mother had the right to see the baby for two hours a month if she remained at Elgen. This was not allowed, however, during May to September, when the women were needed for field work. Children who survived birth and early upbringing in the camp were transferred at the age of seven to a state institution at Talon. From that time, a mother was never allowed to see her child again.

At Kolyma gold and lead is mined, as well as timber cutting. Coal is mined at Vorkuta and Pechora – a huge prison region in the northeastern corner of European Russia where the basin of the Pechora river alone is greater in size than Britain. Throughout Kazakhstan there is coal again. At Norilsk molybdenum is mined. At Kemerovo, in addition to mining nickel, molybdenum and chrome there is timber cutting.

Adam Galinski was a prisoner under Stalin in the huge Pechora complex. Galinski was sentenced – originally to death – for underground activities during the Soviet occupation of his native Poland. For a reason he never discovered, the sentence was commuted to fifteen years *katorga* – the worst form of hard labour.

Most of Galinski's sentence was spent at Vorkuta. It was at Vorkuta that prisoners rebelled after Khrushchev came to power and when he promised relaxations in prison conditions which did not materialize. KGB troops brought in tanks to quell the rioting. There is a women's section at Vorkuta and the women formed a barrier between the rioting men and the tanks. According to Galinski, the KGB drove the tanks over the women: it is estimated that 500 were crushed to death.

In addition to his fifteen-year imprisonment, Galinski was sentenced by judges, who he believes were security officers, to five years' loss of civil rights and permanent settlement at Vorkuta. However, as with his death sentence, there was an official change of heart and he was allowed to emigrate to America. He settled in Washington and it was in the American capital that he gave evidence to a congressional enquiry into prison conditions in Soviet labour camps. Describing his journey to Vorkuta, Galinski said: 'We were transported in cattle cars. At the time I was taken to Vorkuta they organized large convoys for which the ordinary type of prison cars did not suffice. Up to a thousand people were included in a convoy. There were about that many in mine. These people were sent up in cattle cars which were especially reinforced with steel bars, barbed wire and locked from the outside. The train was lit on both sides by very strong searchlights and in the caboose were armed guards who also had dogs. Each car had shelves built on all sides, on which there was room for about thirty men at most. However, they loaded the cars with from fifty to a hundred prisoners. In the centre of each car there was an iron stove, but it was still extremely cold, so cold that the walls inside the cars had ice on them from the humidity of our breath. But we got a kind of comfort out of this, because having so little water we were very thirsty and we used to lick the ice to get some relief.

'In each car there was just a small opening in the floor (for the lavatory) which also served as a point for trading with the prisoners. That is they used to show us bread through the hole and ask for some clothing, saying, for instance, "Give me some shoes and I'll give you some bread" through the same opening.'

The KGB guards and trusties did not provide the food that was officially available for the prisoners. Instead they bartered with them for it, for clothes. And then exchanged the clothing for vodka with people through whose villages they passed. 'This was so well known that at every station on the rail line to Vorkuta there were people waiting already with vodka for such purposes.'

It took Galinski twenty-one days to reach Vorkuta. Throughout his term of imprisonment, he worked in six camps – numbers 7, 12, 14, 25, 26 and one called Abezi. He mined coal.

It is so cold at Vorkuta that the ground is tundra, permanently frozen. There was no native population before the establishment of the camps. Some prisoners had been sentenced to permanent settlement; others were victims of Stalin's mass repopulation.

Galinski's category as political prisoner was the worst. He said, 'People in my category could be shot by a guard under any pretext. At the slightest offence of the camp rules people were put into an "isolator" where they were separated from the external world completely. It had cement walls which became extremely cold since there was no heat. Their clothing was taken away from them and they were left naked in the terrible cold. They were also put in chains.'

Galinski continued, 'A prisoner, after some time in solitary, presents a horrible appearance. He is dirty. He smells of his own excrement. He is generally black and blue from beatings and he is covered with vermin to such an extent that the other prisoners, though they pity him, recoil from him in horror.'

A favoured torture is the Corset. Galinski explained, 'They used to put prisoners in wet shirts in which they put a special chemical which, after some period of drying, made a kind of corset. Even some bones could be broken by the protraction of the corset.'

Such torture has also been described by expelled dissident Vladimir Bukovsky, who spent periods in the Serbsky Institute and other psychiatric hospitals. Bukovsky says it invariably renders the victim unconscious and some die.

Galinski described Russian jails and labour camps as 'hunger, brutality, vermin and treatment that make people lose all of their humanity.' Prisoners were reduced to the level of animals, surviving only by an instinct for self-preservation. In the camps in which Galinski served any prisoner who attempted to escape was brought back in order that other prisoners could see he had been unsuccessful. He was then shot in front of them and the corpse was taken to the main gate and left outside 'so that the work brigades on their way to the mines could see the body.'

In the coal mines of Vorkuta the seams are so narrow men worked prostrated on their stomachs. Knees and elbows were constantly abscessed. Roofs were improperly supported – prisoners often stealing the wooden pillars to burn – and cave-ins were frequent. Illumination was by naked candle flame causing frequent natural gas explosions. When Galinski began his sentence, the work-day was twelve hours, with day and night shifts. Later that was reduced to eight hours, with three shifts working around the clock. The food was 650 grams of bread and twice a day 200 grams of soup – usually with fish – and a few grams of cottonseed oil. The bread was bad and the fish was salted, if not sour. There were never any fresh vegetables. Scurvy was endemic, despite the pine and dwarf willow leaf brew. In the winters prisoners were issued with quilted trousers and waistcoats; shoes were rubber soled, with synthetic uppers. During eight months of the year at Vorkuta the temperature remains at minus 40 to 45 degrees. Occasionally, says Galinski, it dropped as low as 75 degrees below zero.

The Soviet Union is nervous of the criticism of its prison and labour camps, so much so that it has created show camps to which Westerners are taken in order to be convinced that the Russian penal system is a humane one. Galinski said that an entire bogus camp had been built twenty-eight miles outside Moscow, at a place called Kryukovo, to deceive visitors. There were almost 700 'prisoners', KGB men drafted in just before any official visit. People who came to the camp saw prisoners playing table tennis, volley ball and basket ball: there was even a jazz band. They toured immaculate kitchens. Cooks and administrators talked of each prisoner receiving the minimum of 3,600 calories a day. 'Prisoners' were seen in comfortable cells, able to receive as many letters as they liked from relatives, who could also make unlimited prison visits.

Kryukovo, according to Galinski, is a complete sham, a KGB disinformation exercise. So, too, was a visit permitted to the gold-mining camps of Kolyma. The Soviet expert Robert Conquest estimates that between 1931 and 1943 three million prisoners perished in the sub-zero temperatures of this system: an obscene sum equates every ton of Kolyma gold costing 1,000 lives.

In 1944 the Russians allowed the American vice-president, Henry Wallace, to see Kolyma. Galinski tells of a camp being emptied of real prisoners and replaced by security men. Guard towers were taken down and all the barbed wire removed. The stores were filled with food. After his visit, Wallace wrote, 'The Kolyma gold miners are big, husky men who came out to the Far East from European Russia . . . the spirit and meaning of life in Siberia today is certainly not to be compared to that of the old exile days.' Galinski expressed it another way. He said, 'These tourist visits to real camps are a tale out of *A Thousand and One Nights*.' The only difference, of course, is that *A Thousand and One Nights* is a fairy story. Life in the Soviet gulags was a horrifying reality.

Avraham Shifrin is another ex-prisoner who has given evidence before American congressional investigators. He was arrested in 1953, in the Jewish purge which came with Stalin's Doctors' Plot. Shifrin said he spent twenty-five days under interrogation at Lubyanka. He was kept permanently standing and questioned non-stop by a rotating team of six interrogators; if he collapsed, he was doused with water until he got to his feet again. From Lubyanka he was transferred to Lefortovo, another Moscow prison. His cell was four feet by five feet. Shifrin says there were five inches of water and mud on the floor. He had to squat in it because there was no bunk. He kept track of the days – he was there for twenty-eight – by making a mark in the green mould on the wall every time his bread ration was delivered. From Lefortovo he went to Butyrki jail for his trial. He appeared before a military court and was found guilty of spying for Israel and America. He was sentenced to be shot.

He tells of being put into the condemned cell section of Butyrki, close to the Kremlin. Lights were out at ten: executions were at eleven. Shifrin says there was utter silence for that hour, while the condemned men lay awake, listening for the footsteps of the approaching guards, to see if they were to be that night's victims. The chosen men were always silenced by a pear-shaped gag being thrust into their mouths before being taken from their cells. 'Sometimes we heard a last cry as it was being done. Sometimes only a choking sound.'

Shifrin's sentence, like Galinski's, was inexplicably commuted from death to twenty-five years strict labour, five years exile and five years deprivation of rights. Shifrin's first camp was at Chelyabinsk. From the prison to the railway that took him there he was transported in a closed van with a picture on the side of a bear lapping ice cream. There was insufficient room for the last three prisoners to be put into the van; they were hoisted up and thrust to lie on the shoulders of those already standing. From the terminal to Chelyabinsk he was carried in another sealed, disguised van; perhaps appropriately it had the word 'meat' inscribed upon the side. Chelyabinsk was the first of many camp complexes through which Shifrin says he passed. After Chelyabinsk came Novosibirsk. Then Omsk. Ruthlessness was encouraged among camp guards. Robert Conquest makes the point that under Stalin the death penalty was exercised in the camps for anti-Soviet agitation but not for murder. Shifrin attested that in the camps guards were given fifteen days' leave and the right to visit relatives whenever they shot attempted escapees. Inevitably this encouraged guards to provoke escape attempts and then stage ambushes. Around every outside working party, a flag line was created: if a prisoner – even inadvertently – crossed the line he was judged an escapee and shot. A body was not necessary as proof for the leave pass; only an index finger, which was hacked off and then compared, by its print, with the man's prison record.

Ruthlessness bred sadism. Shifrin recounts the fate of one prisoner, in Tayshet, who swore at a guard. The man was stripped naked and tied, straddling a tree. It was the time of the year when poisonous mosquito and gnats, called *moshky*, were swarming: even working prisoners were allowed protective gauze nets. By nightfall the naked man had been stung to death, his body a bloated red corpse.

Shifrin describes in detail the 'especially strict' labour camp to which he was transferred in 1960. It was number 410, at Vikhorevka, near Bratsk. The camp, looking out from the inside, was constructed from coils of barbed wire, beyond which there was a barbed wire fence about nine feet high. Then came a ploughed earth strip about three yards wide. After the open space there was a wooden fence some twelve feet high, with three feet of barbed wire on top. Then more ploughed earth. After this second open space there was a further nine-foot tall barbed wire fence. And finally an outer protection of seven coils of barbed wire. At each corner was a watch tower.

At camp 410 cells were twelve feet by six feet and contained twelve prisoners. There was a common bunk, on the window side. There was an open lavatory pot. Condensation from their breath froze on the floor. They were allowed 675 grams of black bread – 'like clay' – every day and a soup of rotting cabbages and a small piece of fish.

Sick or insane prisoners were not moved from the cells containing other prisoners, but left to rant and scream, frequently defecating or urinating on the floors. Shifrin talked of a Sunday at camp 410 when a group of women were being escorted from the women's section to the showers. Among them were a number of nuns. They asked to be allowed to shower the following day because they did not want to violate the sabbath. Shifrin said, 'The KGB guards stripped them naked and dragged them by their hair through the snow to the washroom.'

Shifrin's is not the only account of nuns being subjected to brutality because of their refusal on religious grounds to obey orders on holy days. In her book *Eleven Years in Soviet Prisons*, Elinor Lipper, a Stalin prisoner in Kolyma, wrote: 'On all Sundays and church holy days they [the nuns] would go to the lockup. Neither persuasion, threats, mockery nor physical punishment could force them to work on the Lord's Days. They ate their slender punishment rations and sang their songs. They were beaten. Their skirts were tied over their heads and sometimes they were tied together by the hair. It did not help. On the following Sunday they allowed themselves to be pushed into the lockup as patiently, submissively and unflinchingly as ever.'

Shifrin was moved from Vikhorevka, via a re-assembly camp, to another especially strict camp at Udarnyy. There were seventy prisoners in each cattle car of the prison train, constructed so that there were guard towers giving an elevated view of the trucks. Other guards, with dogs, patrolled the corridors. Beneath each car was a steel rake, the teeth of which cleared the track by only inches: prisoners sometimes broke through the floor of the car and tried to drop to freedom. If they attempted it from this train, they would have been impaled. The journey took six days; the prisoners were allowed a cup of water twice a day, bread and salt fish.

In Udarnyy each cell was ten feet by nine feet. Seven men lived there; on the communal bunk it meant each man had a space of six and a half inches by thirty inches. During the summer, the prisoners made bricks by hand. In the winter, when it was impossible to work, they were locked up permanently in the cells. There was a lavatory pot at one end, a table at the other. In the minuscule corridor remaining, two men at a time would attempt to exercise, while the remaining five squatted on the bunk.

CHAPTER TWELVE

THE GERM FACTORIES

In 1972 the Soviet Union signed the Biological Weapons Convention with the United States of America, outlawing the development, production or stockpiling of biological warfare agents. The convention came into effect in 1975 and has been ratified by 112 nations. Russia ignores it with the contempt with which it treats the United Nations and the proper diplomatic function of its embassies throughout the West. On balance, it must be said that America shows matching contempt. The Pentagon has operational plans to equip their 2,000-mile capability Cruise missile with chemical germ warheads. Above and below the ground in Utah are vast stocks of VX gas manufactured before President Nixon declared America opposed to biological warfare. There are plans to equip the European-based F-111 fighter with rockets fitted with germ warheads. And America has developed the binary weapon, a shell or rocket into which two separate containers of chemicals are fitted. Apart, both containers are harmless: and only one container is installed in the factory. The second container is not inserted until the moment of firing. During trajectory, the separating walls of the two containers break, the liquid mixes and the result is a killing germ poison called GB.

In the Soviet Union there are germ-warfare poison laboratories and manufacturing factories at Kirov, Sverdlovsk, Saratov, Kaluga, Suzdal, Moscow, Novosibirsk and Kalinin. Evidence has been given to American congressmen that at Wrangel Island, deep within the Arctic Circle, human experiments with some of these germs have been carried out upon labour-camp prisoners.

These installations are controlled by the Seventh Directorate of the Soviet General Staff and guarded by both KGB and GRU soldiers. There is also a Chief Chemical Directorate of the Ministry of Defence under which experiments are conducted. The Seventh Directorate is headed by Colonel General Yefim Ivanovich Smirnov. Vaccine development is being conducted under the direction of the Soviet deputy minister of Health, Burgasov, who works in close co-operation with the KGB. It is estimated by Western intelligence that at least 125 microbiologists, epidemiologists, zoologists and specialists in communicable diseases work at Kirov. Surrounding the Kirov plant are two rows of reinforced concrete walls. The first wall encloses the scientific research laboratory and is guarded by the GRU. The second wall encompasses the production unit. These contain storage vats in which huge quantities of infectious bacillus are kept. Killer germs stored here include plague, tularemia, tetanus, anthrax and yellow fever. This second enclosure is guarded by KGB personnel.

At Kirov entomologists are experimenting with mosquitoes as a possible method of spreading germs. At Suzdal the secret bacteriological institute is housed in a former monastery. Here prisoner microbiologists work under the control of KGB guards. Two programmes of experiments involve plague and tularemia.

In March 1980 there was an explosion at Sverdlovsk. The cause is unknown in the West but it is believed to have involved only one storage container. At once KGB troops and scientists were drafted to the area and an extremely painful type of vaccination was enforced upon the civilian population. Fortunately the explosion – at the institute known as number 19 – was on the south side of the town and the wind was blowing in a southerly direction, taking the cloud of poison which rose into the air away from it.

Despite this wind and the vaccination precautions, a minimum of 1,000 people – workers in a nearby brick factory and the occupants of an outlying village – are known to have died from the effects of a particularly virulent form of anthrax.

As with the ricin that killed Georgi Markov and the thallium which reduced Nikolai Khokhlov to a Frankenstein-like monster, the KGB appears always to want to make a deadly germ even more lethal. With anthrax that would hardly seem necessary. During World War II, British scientists carried out anthrax experiments on the Scottish island of Gruinard. Thirty-seven years later Gruinard is still a prohibited place of barbed wire and landing barriers. The anthrax germs on Gruinard – a high explosive shell to an atom bomb in comparison to the Sverdlovsk infection – are undiminished in lethal strength.

In the Penkovsky Papers the executed Western spy Oleg Penkovsky talks of a gas developed at a laboratory near Moscow that is without colour, taste or smell. He describes it as 'very effective and highly toxic.' With an obvious implication, it is named American. Penkovsky says that all Russian artillery units are supplied with chemical warfare shells and trained regularly in their use. The decision to utilize them is relegated to the local military commander. He continues, 'And let there be no doubt: if hostilities should erupt the Soviet Army would use chemical weapons against its opponents.'

In March 1982, the United States claimed in a 32-page report to the United Nations and to Congress that since 1975 more than 10,000 people had been killed in nearly 400 Russian chemical-warfare attacks in three countries. The report itemized those countries as Laos, Cambodia and Afghanistan.

The Deputy Secretary of State, Walter Stoessel – the man who had suffered a Soviet radiation assault when he was U.S. ambassador in Moscow – said, 'The Soviet Union and its allies are flagrantly and repeatedly violating international laws and agreements. If the world fails to halt this activity, it will have little chance to prevent its repetition in other lands against other peoples.'

Russia immediately labelled the report, a declassified CIA assessment, as 'dirty lies' and pointedly added, 'The world has not forgotten that tens of thousands of chemical agents were dropped over Vietnam, Laos and Cambodia in the years of U.S. aggression in Indo-China.'

Although the report contained evidence from supposed survivors of chemical attacks, doctors who treated them and defectors who claimed such assaults were being made, the American administration was forced to admit that it possessed no direct evidence, such as a Soviet marked canister. Despite the absence of such evidence, however, America insisted Soviet involvement was 'inescapable'.

According to the U.S. document the chemicals used included nerve gases, irritants, incapacitants and lethal mycotoxins. The primary toxins identified were trichothecenes and biologically active fungal substances that cause acute respiratory and gastro-intestinal diseases. American aircraft captured during the Vietnam war were used to drop the chemicals, claimed the report.

The CIA document itemized 261 attacks in Laos and said 6,504 people had died. Survivors talked of being enveloped in 'red gas' or being covered by a 'yellow cloud'. In Cambodia there were 124 attacks between 1978 and 1981 and a total of 981 people died. In Afghanistan, there had been forty-seven chemical attacks against the rebel Mujahedeen forces since 1979, killing 3,042 people.

Germ warfare experimentation is not the only sort of research being carried out by KGB scientists at Novosibirsk. Under the aegis of the Soviet Academy of Science there is Special Department 8. This department is investigating parapsychology – thought transference. There have been experiments with animals, giving kittens electric shocks to see if their mothers register any reaction three floors away, and upon humans. Under television surveillance people in separate rooms attempt thought exchange, some with remarkable success.

Former Soviet scientist August Stern, now an émigré in the United States, worked for three years at Science City in Novosibirsk, on experiments carried out to find a physical basis for psychic energy, known as psi particles. He was attached to the Institute for Automation and Electronomy run by Vitaly Perov. Research into thought transference is also being conducted by military and naval scientists at Leningrad and Moscow.

Since 1960, the Soviet Union has opened seven new laboratories to study parapsychology. In Moscow Viktor Ada-menko, working with a psychic subject named Alla Vinogra-dova, has succeeded with telekinesis – the use of mental electrical energy – in moving objects weighing as much as 100 grams on a table top. Western intelligence experts believe that a classified instrument capable of measuring the electrical signals known to be emitted from the brain has already been developed within the Soviet Union. The director at the GRU-controlled laboratory in the Soviet Scientific Technical Society of Radiotechnique and Electrocommunication is I. M. Kogan. He is regarded as the foremost Soviet scientist in the field of parapsychology. Another leader in what the Soviet Union consider to be a science is Gennadii Aleksandrovich Sergeyev.

Working on the theory that mental telepathy is possible through the medium of electromagnetic radiation, they conduct training sessions lasting for three hours, three times a week; data indicates – certainly in the opinion of Adamenko – that women are better subjects than men.

At the parapsychology laboratories experimentation is also being conducted on automatic hypnosis. Scientists have created a device codenamed Lida – an acronym for a remote-controlled therapeutic apparatus – for automatic hypnosis. It emits pulsating light, heat and sound on VHF.

There is KGB interest in the experiments at the Leningrad Institute for Brain Research of L. L. Vasiliev, who is attempting to use telepathy over a long distance to influence subjects. Similar long-distance telepathic communication is being attempted by Kogan, who is attached to the Moscow Board of the Popov Society. He is also attempting to use mind control in sending a mental suggestion in which a recipient attempts to identify an object over a short distance. Another test programme involves mentally awakening a subject who has been put to sleep hypnotically over a short distance without using any other stimulus.

In 1977 *Los Angeles Times* correspondent Robert Toth was arrested, jailed and then expelled from the Soviet Union for writing about the Russian interest in parapsychology. He was accused of having received 'state secrets'. Scientists attached to Western intelligence agencies – predominantly the American and French – believe the Soviet research is directed at intelligence use. The French in particular theorize that the Russians are experimenting with parapsychology for espionage use, for thought control and surveillance.

The parapsychology experiments are the ultimate in the KGB attempts to control the minds of the people. In 1917, Lenin said, 'The state is an instrument for coercion.'

After sixty-five years, the KGB has become that instrument. The Soviet state is wielding it like the sword that forms part of the KGB emblem.

CHAPTER THIRTEEN

THE ELITE AND THEIR EFFICIENCY

Internally, with its labour camps and restrictive laws and its babble of informers, the KGB has created the most effective police state in the world. Certainly there is dissent, from a few brave ethnic Russians, from Jews and from some of the republics, particularly from the Ukraine and Georgia. But compared to the size of the country and its population, that opposition is minimal, magnified out of proportion by Western publicity of a protest in a Moscow square or the arrest of a nationalist in the provinces. The hunger strike protest of Nobel Peace Prize winner, Andrei Dmitrivich Sakharov and his wife in December 1981 ended in a KGB capitulation by allowing Liza Alekseyeva to emigrate to America to join Sakharov's stepson, whom she had married by proxy. But that does not indicate any relaxation of KGB oppression. It indicates, rather, the advantage of the fame of the inventor of the Soviet hydrogen bomb. Sakharov was too well known internationally to be allowed to die. For every one Sakharov there are a hundred unknowns whose protests are mercilessly crushed.

Externally the KGB is not as successful as the amount of money spent and the effort expended dictate that it should be. But it is still effective. Complemented as it is by its satellite services, it could hardly fail to be: a vacuum cleaner can collect more than a handbrush and pan, although the latter often succeeds in doing a more thorough job.

Some intelligence experts who have helped me with this book, particularly one American, consider the KGB to be a constantly underestimated threat to the freedom of the West. Others subscribe to the dinosaur theory.

The reality comes between the two. The biggest spy machine for the gathering of secret information which the world has ever seen should be regarded properly with the caution befitting a monster but not the hysteria accorded one that will crush underfoot everything in its path.

The Soviet Union needs the KGB because without it there would not be a Soviet Union. But why do people become part of a monster apparatus – an organization they know to be reviled and despised throughout the country? The first answer is fear; the second human nature. Like the universities and academies of the West, the institutes of learning in the Soviet Union are recruiting grounds for their security service. To refuse the offer, as some do, is to be branded as effectively as a tattooed dissenter in the labour camp, someone to be regarded for the rest of his or her life not as a favoured member of Russian society but as a constant object of KGB scrutiny and harassment.

Vladimir Titov was such a man. Initially he accepted KGB employment, working within the state security organization from 1956 until 1962 and rising to the rank of first lieutenant. In 1962, disgusted at what he was daily called upon to do against his fellow countrymen, he did the unthinkable. He resigned. Titov, a Jew, was at once regarded as an enemy of the state. For the next twelve years he was shunted between two prisons, one forced labour camp and three mental institutions, one of them the prison hospital at Sychevka. Upon his release in 1974, he applied to emigrate to Israel. The KGB, intimating a deal, asked Titov to expose friends whom it regarded as fellow dissidents. He refused. In March 1981, he was arrested in the West Siberian region of Tyumen, where he lived, and charged with 'anti-Soviet propaganda'. Once more he was interned in a local mental hospital, this time upon an imposed and enforced programme of drug treatment. At the time of writing Vladimir Titov, a KGB man who dared to say, no, is still incarcerated.

For those who do not rebel or actively seek to belong to the KGB – to be a Chekist – is to be one of an élite, a member of the favoured class in the Soviet Union. In a country of permanent housing shortage and apartment-sharing between families, a KGB officer can always obtain accommodation. He – or she – has access to concessionary stores and from them to drink, food and goods denied the ordinary Russian. The menu of the basement canteens in Dzerzhinsky Square list foods unavailable in any Moscow shop. The apartment of

Yuri Andropov, the recent head of the KGB, in Kutuzovsky Prospect has foreign, not Russian furniture; he stopped short of the useless blinking telephone of Victor Louis but his stereo equipment is equally elaborate.

A KGB man is *someone*; he is different from the rest.

Vladimir Feltsman is not. He is a non-person, sentenced to oblivion by the KGB. Feltsman is a pianist. When he was fifteen he won first prize at the Concertina International Competition in Prague. At nineteen he won first prize at the Margaret Long International Competition in Paris. There the music critic of *Le Figaro* described him as 'extraordinarily brilliant'. It was not an isolated opinion. *L'Aurore*, another French newspaper, said, 'He must be counted among the great musicians of the world.'

Russia recognized its piano genius. Tikhon Khrennikov, first secretary of the Union of Soviet Composers, wrote in the *Sovetskaya Kultura* that Feltsman was 'a pianist of extraordinarily vivid gifts, with a big future.' It appeared to be a valid judgment. Feltsman toured extensively in the Soviet Union and Eastern Europe. His recordings of Chopin, Schumann, Schubert and Brahms were sold throughout France, West Germany, the United States and Japan. In 1977, although his biologist wife Anna was refused permission to accompany him, Feltsman was allowed a tour of Japan. The following year, with Anna still kept in the Soviet Union, he gave a programme of recitals in France. In both Japan and France the eulogies continued.

At 10 a.m. on 23 May 1979, Feltsman went to the assistant manager of the Moscow State Philharmonic, where he was a soloist, and asked for references necessary to apply for an exit visa for himself and Anna to emigrate to Israel. At noon the same day Feltsman received a telephone call from a friend at the State Television and Radio station telling him they had been ordered to remove every recording Feltsman had ever made from their archives and never to play them again.

A fortnight later Feltsman was scheduled to play, as a soloist, with the Moscow Philharmonic in the Great Hall of the Moscow Conservatory. Posters advertised the concert throughout the Russian capital. At 3 p.m. on the day of the concert squads of men toured Moscow, erasing Feltsman's name with black marking ink. At 5 p.m., Feltsman was told his concert was cancelled. Within a month, all records and tapes of anything Feltsman had ever done were removed from Soviet stores and shops.

Since that time repeated applications from Feltsman for him and his wife to be allowed to emigrate to Israel have been refused. Feltsman feared his ability as a pianist was being endangered by his inability to perform publicly. Eighteen months after he ceased, officially, to exist as a Soviet musician, a series of solo recitals were arranged in six of the smaller cities in the Ukraine. The first was to be in the town of Sumy.

Feltsman, hopefully, made the wearisome journey. He was met at Sumy by the director of the local booking office who said that without posters advertising Feltsman's appearance, he had not been able to make any arrangements for the recital. The posters are printed in Moscow. They had not arrived.

The KGB does not need assassination, jail, prison or concentration camp to destroy someone it regards as an enemy of the state.

ODYSSEY OF RAOUL WALLENBERG

By 1944 Germany was already losing World War II. Hitler's divisions were being driven out of Russia. After the victories in North Africa, the Allies invaded Europe from the south and forced Italy into surrender. In March, just three months before the Normandy landings, the desperate Nazis occupied Hungary. The country was important to them: strategically they wanted a buffer against the Russian advance from the east. But there was another reason. Regardless of the war turning against him, Hitler was determined to conclude his Final Solution and rid Europe of Jews. In Hungary there were 800,000 Jews. Adolph Eichmann, the Third Reich's most efficient Jewish exterminator, was entrusted with the job of liquidating them.

Eichmann was as obedient as ever. Aided by the Arrow Cross, the country's Fascists, he began the deportations, initially in the countryside. Eichmann organized train convoys to Auschwitz on a round-the-clock timetable and when the transportation system became overloaded he ordered that Jews be forced to march to the Austrian border, to rail assembly points. Children, old people and women who collapsed through exhaustion or exposure were shot and their bodies left along the roadside. Eichmann was to succeed in destroying 100,803 Hungarian Jews.

The Western governments were aware that the Nazis had a policy of Final Solution, although it was not until the gates of Belsen, Dachau and Auschwitz were opened at the end of the war that even they appreciated its complete and enormous obscenity. When, in 1944, the facts about Hungary leaked out, there was an immediate response from the World Jewish Congress. They began to put pressure on the government of Franklin Roosevelt to prevent any further genocide.

Roosevelt had already established the War Refugee Board to save – through neutral countries – Jews and others from Nazi persecution. Sweden was a neutral country. On the advisory committee of the Board's division in Stockholm was a Jew called Koloman Lauer. He had a business partner whose name was Raoul Wallenberg.

By June of 1944 Eichmann had begun the round-up of the 264,803 Jews living in the Hungarian capital of Budapest. The understaffed Swedish embassy there was issuing protective passports but the Nazi extermination efficiency was making its efforts appear pitiful. What was needed, decided the Refugee Board, was a man who could match Eichmann. By the end of June it had found him. He was Raoul Wallenberg.

Wallenberg was neither a diplomat, nor a Jew; by religion he was a Lutheran. He was an aristocrat, born into the favoured luxury of a banking family who have been called the Rockefellers of Sweden. An accomplished linguist – as well as Swedish he spoke French, German, English and Russian – Wallenberg studied architecture at the University of Michigan; he graduated with the honours prize at the age of twenty-one. He toured Mexico and South Africa. In 1936 he worked for a Dutch bank in Haifa. It was there, for the first time, that he heard how Jews were treated, even in the pre-war streets of Munich and Berlin.

He was a man of medium build, his dark hair already receding. He had a prominent nose and dark eyes that were memorable. People who met him said there was a passion in them – surprising for someone who outwardly appeared gentle and soft spoken.

At the end of June 1944 this passionate but ordinary-looking man volunteered to take temporary diplomatic status and go to the Hungarian capital for one purpose only: to save the lives of Jews. His step-sister, Ms Nina Lagergren recalls: 'I always felt my brother would do something very special with his life. My family were not surprised at his act. We knew what he did was the greatest challenge of his life. It took hold of him.' There was no way of predicting, in June 1944, what the appalling cost would be to Raoul Wallenberg.

Wallenberg reached Budapest on 9 July 1944. He was thirty-two. He wore a long, leather coat over a jerkin. A sleeping bag was rolled against one of his two rucksacks. In the other was money provided by the Refugee Board. Later that cash supplied by the United States was to prove disastrous.

On the Pest side of the Danube Wallenberg bought thirty-two apartments. He draped them conspicuously with the Swedish flag and declared them diplomatically inviolate from Arrow Cross or Germans. There was no furniture because it would have occupied space. And Wallenberg wanted all the space he could get. He covered the floors with mattresses and crowded Jews in with a minimum of twenty to a room, sometimes more. At one stage it was estimated he crammed 15,000 people into his apartments.

Wallenberg was as good an organizer as Eichmann. From the Jews he saved he created a bureaucracy of 355 clerks and assistants, forty doctors, two 'hospitals' and a soup kitchen. It was not enough for the passionate-eyed man.

At the Swedish embassy Wallenberg designed and printed a totally false and illegal protective passport, a Schutzpass. It carried the symbolic three crown stamp of Sweden and the ambassador's signature. To the bureaucratically minded Nazis, documentation was everything: Wallenberg issued the Schutzpass to any Jew who could reach the embassy but that was not easy. The Nazis created walled-in ghetto 'prisons' for the 200,000 Jews still in Budapest, which facilitated the daily assembly for the week-long cattle truck journeys to extermination. Jews were only allowed beyond the ghetto between 4 p.m. and 5 p.m.; rarely was the queue outside the embassy less than half-a-mile long.

Still Wallenberg was not satisfied. Almost daily he went to the railway terminals, bluffing and bullying his way past guards and actually entering cattle cars crowded with whimpering, dejected people convinced that they were about to die. He made them produce any document printed in Hungarian, which the Nazis could not read, and then insisted to the Germans that it was proof of Swedish nationality and that the holders were under his protection.

He even physically confronted Eichmann. At a dinner party, he said to the Nazi, 'You have to face it. You've lost the war. Why not give up now?' Eichmann's reply was that he had a job to do. Then he said to Wallenberg, 'Don't think you are immune just because you are a diplomat and a neutral.'

Within days, Wallenberg's car was crushed out of recognition by a German lorry. But Wallenberg was not in the vehicle. Recognizing it for the assassination attempt it was, Wallenberg once more confronted Eichmann. As the Swede left his office, Eichmann said, 'I will try again.'

But killing Jews was more important. The Arrow Cross and Germans started snatch raids on Wallenberg's safe houses when he was not there to oppose them. Wallenberg stole SS uniforms, dressed Aryan-looking Jews in them and frightened the attackers into believing the Nazi élitist corps had established a guard.

With the relentless approach of the Russians, the Nazis became frantic to finish the Jewish liquidation. Jews were marched to the banks of the Danube and shot in the back so that their bodies pitched into the water. Again Wallenberg intruded, sometimes standing at rifle or pistol point while Jews scrambled any printed piece of paper from their pockets to claim Swedish protection. He drove along the snow and ice-packed death-march routes, issuing passports to those he could, and when the documents ran out, food for those he could not save.

By January 1945, the Russians were on the outskirts of Budapest. Bombs and shells hammered the city into rubble: from the Berlin bunker came the order that Budapest had to be fought for, street by street. Exasperated by the Jew-saving activities of the Swedish embassy, the Germans shelled it, forcing the diplomats into hiding on the Buda side of the river. Fellow Swedes beseeched Wallenberg to quit his 'safe' houses on the Pest side and hide with them until liberation.

'The Jews need me more,' he said. On 10 January, Wallenberg discovered just how much. That was the day he learned that the hurriedly retreating Germans intended resolving the problem of the 70,000 Jews now concentrated into one general ghetto by sending in killer squads of Waffen SS – fully militarized combat formations of the SS – and the Arrow Cross gunmen while putting a hundred policemen around the ghetto boundary to ensure that not one single Jew escaped slaughter.

By now Wallenberg was on the SS death list. Unable to confront them as openly as he had in the preceding months, he got an emissary through to the overall commander of the SS troops, General August Schmidthuber. The message was the same as it had been to Eichmann: that the war was lost. And then came the threat. If the Germans carried out their intention to massacre the Jews in the ghetto, Wallenberg would personally testify at Schmidthuber's trial for war crimes and see that he was hanged. For several moments Schmidthuber considered the ultimatum and then cancelled the order. That confrontation on the night of 10 January brought the number of Jews personally saved from death by Raoul Wallenberg to 100,000. No one person – not even a Western government – saved more.

The following day the Germans blew up the bridges across the Danube, linking the two sides of the city, Buda and Pest, to one another. Wallenberg was trapped on the eastern side. It was from the east that the Russians were advancing. They arrived on 13 January. With them was the organization today known as the KGB. Wallenberg's reaction, naturally, was that the Russians were liberators. He had thousands of Jews to feed and American money with which to buy the food. Wallenberg went out to meet the Russians.

On 16 January, the Russian Foreign Ministry officially informed the Swedish embassy in Moscow, 'Mr Wallenberg was found in Budapest and taken under the protection of the Russian army.' Twenty-four hours later, under Russian guard, Wallenberg arrived at the 'safe house' office on the Pest side of the river from which, over the preceding seven months, he had planned his momentous rescue of 100,000 Jews. With him was his driver, Kilmos Langfelder, one of those he had kept from the gas chambers. Wallenberg explained to his Jewish helpers that he wanted money to buy the provisions they needed and documents to prove to the Russians what he had been doing. He told them he was going to Debrecen, 140 miles east of Budapest, to meet Russian Marshal Rodion Malinovsky personally. Later, as Minister for Defence, Malinovsky was responsible for the military espionage branch of Soviet intelligence, the GRU. In 1945 he was already a member.

Wallenberg collected what he wanted and moved to leave. He stopped suddenly by the door, turning to those still inside the room. Then, chillingly prophetic, he said: 'I don't know whether I'm going as a prisoner or a guest.'

And then Raoul Wallenberg vanished.

For thirty-seven years, the fate of Raoul Wallenberg has been a mystery. Ignoring their Foreign Ministry communication of 6 January 1945, the Russians steadfastly denied any knowledge of his whereabouts. Then in 1957, they said that he had died of a heart attack in cell 123 of Lubyanka prison, in July 1947.

It was a lie.

For more than thirty years Raoul Wallenberg has been shunted through the labour and concentration camps of the KGB and its predecessors, a potential personal embarrassment to Russian leader Leonid Brezhnev. From 1941 to 1946 Brezhnev commanded the political department of Russia's 18th Army. It was Brezhnev's responsibility to issue arrest orders for suspected spies. And it was as such that the Russians regarded Wallenberg, with his readily available source of American money. To the Russians – then and now – it was unthinkable that anyone would have risked his life and done what Wallenberg did to save Jews. Among the documents that Wallenberg took to meet Malinovsky at Debrecen – the special train carrying Wallenberg did not even stop, but went straight on through Hungary and into Russia – were proposals for the large-scale rehabilitation of Jews after the war. To the Russians – and to Brezhnev – they represented plans for a mammoth Western spy network that was to permeate the countries of Europe. The Soviet Union had intentions for espionage networks of its own in Europe.

Lieutenant Yaakov Leontovich Lakhotski-Menaker was attached to the 18th Army. At reunions in 1976 and 1977 he learned of Brezhnev's personal order from the man who carried out Wallenberg's arrest. He was a Tartar captain whose name Menaker recalled as Aminiev. When he seized Wallenberg, Aminiev was already the holder of the Aleksandr Nevsky Order. As a reward for his arrest of the Swede he expected to be made a Hero of the Soviet Union. He was never awarded the decoration.

For over three decades the Swedes have made vacillating, ineffectual attempts to trace Wallenberg. In November 1981, they had an ideal, although diplomatically questionable, opportunity of imposing pressure upon the Kremlin when the atomic warhead-equipped Whisky class submarine 137 ran aground on a spying mission deep within Swedish territorial waters near Karlskrona. Aboard was a Russian crew of fifty-seven officers and men. Other countries – including Switzerland – have forced the release of Soviet detained and imprisoned nationals by seizing Russians and demanding exchanges. Sweden spent a week extracting meaningless statements from Moscow, which the Swedes immediately dismissed as untrue, and then towed the Soviet vessel to freedom in the Baltic.

Now America is taking up the search for Raoul Wallenberg. In October 1981, Wallenberg was made an honorary citizen of the United States: the only other foreigner to whom the honour has been extended was Sir Winston Churchill in 1963.

Honorary citizenship means that Washington has a diplomatic lever to use upon Moscow. President Reagan has indicated that he means to use it. At the ceremony attended by Ms. Lagergren, Reagan said the evidence was sufficiently strong to believe that even now Wallenberg was still alive. In Jerusalem the commemorative monument to the six million Jews who died in the Holocaust is called Yad Vashem: leading to its museum is an avenue of carob trees, each one named after a Gentile who risked his life to save a Jew. One is planted in memory of Raoul Wallenberg. Reagan told Ms Lagergren, 'We are going to do everything in our power to see your brother can sit in the shade of those trees.'

The evidence which the President was referring to started to emerge in 1951. That was the year the Italian diplomat Claudio de Mohr was released from Russian imprisonment. A trained, reliable observer, de Mohr provided a perfect description of Wallenberg, who had occupied cell 151 in Moscow's Lefortovo prison: Mohr's had been cell 152. They established contact by tapping in morse code on the cell wall, speaking in German. Wallenberg recounted the details of his Budapest arrest and subsequent imprisonment. From Mohr's account after his release, the Swedish premier, Tage Erlander, personally raised Wallenberg's imprisonment with Khrushchev in 1956, at a meeting in Moscow. According to

Erlander, Khrushchev went red in the face and shouted at the Swedish premier, 'I don't want to hear that name again! I know nothing about this person and I don't want to know anything about him. If you mention him again I will break off negotiations.'

If Khrushchev disclaimed knowledge of Wallenberg, others did not. Six German prisoners of war were repatriated with accounts of either sharing a cell with him or talking to him through wall tapping. In 1961 Professor Nanna Svartz attended a medical conference in Moscow. She spoke, in German, to Russian professor, A. L. Myasnikov, about Wallenberg. Myasnikov said that Wallenberg was a patient in a mental hospital and that he had personally treated him. When Sweden asked for an explanation, Moscow said it was untrue and Myasnikov later denied that his conversation with Professor Svartz had ever occurred.

The British businessman and spy Greville Wynne – arrested and put on trial with Oleg Penkovsky – encountered in Lubyanka prison a man who shouted, 'I am a Swede' and whom Wynne subsequently came to believe was Wallenberg. After being allowed to emigrate from Russia to Israel, a Polish Jew, Abraham Kalinsky, told investigators probing Wallenberg's fate that he saw the Swede three times during periods of Soviet imprisonment. The last occasion was in October 1959 in Moscow's Vladimir prison.

In 1973 Haim Moshinski, in a sworn affidavit from his home in Israel, provided evidence to a House of Representatives investigating committee of seeing Wallenberg in a notorious camp at Wrangel Island. Moshinski described Wallenberg as 'a handsome, educated man'.

Wrangel Island – *Ostrov Vrangelya* in Russian – is eighty miles northeast of Siberia, an appropriately shaped teardrop seventy-five miles long and forty-five miles wide, deep within the Arctic Circle. The temperature is never above freezing: sometimes it reaches 70 degrees below. At one end of the island there is a training camp for GRU agents. Human experiments are alleged to have been conducted on this island.

There are three separate labour camps. On one there is an atomic reactor and it has been alleged to American politicians that tests on the effect of radiation upon the body are conducted on men and women. In the second camp research is carried out into the strengths and efficiency of poisons, particularly those developed on a large scale and stockpiled for possible use in germ warfare. In this second camp it was also claimed that research was made into human survival, with victims tested until they died and fed on the minimum requirement of food and liquid intake. The third also conducts survival experiments. These are predominantly on submarine escape, to test from varying depths escape suits being considered for use by Soviet submariners, and to observe the influence upon the body of pressure. In the sub-zero temperature of the water, the suits are also examined for warmth to see how long a person can survive before inevitable death. Experiments are also carried out on oxygen deprivation, clinically 'killing' a person by drowning and then investigating the possibility of resuscitation by medical equipment carried in Soviet submarines. Amazingly, Wallenberg survived his term of imprisonment at Wrangel Island.

The next positive sighting of Wallenberg came in 1977. That year Mrs Anna Bilder received a telephone call in Tel Aviv from her father, Jan Kaplan, former administrator of an operatic *conservatoire* in Moscow. He had just been released from a Moscow jail. The conversation turned to survival and Kaplan described to his daughter how, despite the crushing, brutal conditions in the penal institutions, there were frequent cases of prisoners living for surprisingly long periods. 'In fact,' said Kaplan over the fading telephone link, 'I met a Swede in the Butyrki prison in Moscow who has survived thirty years.'

Mrs Bilder did not hear from her family again for almost two years. In July 1979, she learned why. Her mother, Mrs Eugenia Kaplan, got a letter to her from Russia. In it Mrs Kaplan said her husband had attempted to smuggle out an earlier letter detailing Wallenberg's imprisonment through Jews he met in a synagogue. But KGB men from the Jewish department of the Fifth Chief Directorate seized it. Already Jan Kaplan had served a further year and a half in Lefortovo and Lubyanka prisons in Moscow, because of what he had tried to disclose. A distraught Mrs Kaplan wrote of her husband: 'I have now lost all hope of ever seeing him again.'

In 1979 a Russian emigrant to Israel detailed a party at the home of a drunken KGB officer, during which the man said: 'I have a Swede under my charge in Lubyanka who's been inside for over thirty years.'

Wallenberg was still alive in 1980 – according to evidence before an international tribunal which assembled in Stockholm to consider evidence. That year he was incarcerated in a prison in Leningrad. Today if he is still alive, Raoul Wallenberg, whose life-saving work in wartime Budapest was called by President Reagan an accomplishment of 'biblical proportions', would be seventy years old.

The American state of Alaska faces Siberia, across the Bering Strait and the Chukchi Sea. From the Alaskan coastline there juts a promontory, pointing like an accusing finger at Wrangel Island. By bitter irony, it is called Point Hope. Unless America moves with greater speed and more force than Sweden has done for nearly forty years, hope will be fading for Raoul Wallenberg, a man who fought one sort of bestiality and because of it has endured another for thirty-seven years from the KGB and its forerunners.

THE LANGUAGE OF SPYING

Mole, to describe a spy who has burrowed his way deep into the fabric of a rival intelligence service, is such a descriptive word. So, too, is *sleeper*, to mean an agent who has been implanted into a country for an indeterminate time, waiting to be roused into action. Alas, they remain where they fit so well, on the pages of spy fiction rather than on a message pad for cipher transmission to Dzerzhinsky Square, although I have seen the word *sleeper* used in a question to a defecting spy, who answered, understanding its meaning.

The lexicon that follows is drawn from the evidence of such defectors and from communications intercepted by Western intelligence agencies.

Agent of influence. Suborned or ideologically committed people occupying a position within a country where they can affect public opinion in favour of the Soviet Union: politicians, journalists, political commentators, trade union leaders and university academics, for example.

Avanpost. A foreign spy cell, frequently involving two or more networks.

Boyevaya. A Combat group, usually from the GRU. Trained killers employed upon assassinations.

Centre. KGB headquarters, 2, Dzerzhinsky Square, Moscow.

Corporations. Communist parties of foreign countries.

Corporants (or *corporators*). Members of foreign communist parties.

Cut-out. A KGB middleman, often not actively engaged in the physical gathering of espionage, employed as liaison between a cell and the KGB *rezident* within the Soviet embassy. The purpose is to create undetectable cells and at the same time reduce the risk of embarrassing publicity if the network is discovered.

Dead drop (see *Post Box*). In Russian *tainik*, a hiding place for agent communication.

Director. Moscow controller.

Dubok. A hiding place.

Doctor. The police.

Double. Agent working for two sides at the same time.

Flap and seal artist. Experts who can, undetected, open and reseal documents.

Good Services Assistance. In either direction, between a KGB legal and illegal.

Hospital. A prison.

Illegals. KGB spies placed in a country with false identities, to work independent of any Soviet embassy or consulate.

Illness. Arrest or detection.

In the net (see *Nash*). Used to refer to someone who has carried out an incriminating act of espionage, is from that moment susceptible to blackmail and therefore committed to work for the KGB.

Legals. KGB and GRU personnel assigned with diplomatic, and therefore legal, status to a Russian embassy in a foreign country.

Legend. A cover story, supplied to illegals, enabling them to live undetected within a foreign country.

Music box. Radio transmitter.

Musician. Wireless operator.

Neighbour. In Russian *sosed*, a complementary intelligence system: thus the GRU are neighbours of the KGB, as are any of the satellite intelligence systems it uses so extensively.

Nash. Literal translation is 'ours'. It means an agent either suborned or committed to the KGB through ideology.

Novator. An acronym of *novye*, which means new, and *torit*, to level or flatten. It is applied to a newly recruited agent in a foreign country.

Nurses (and *shepherds*). KGB personnel accompanying Russians on overseas visits.

Post box. Literally that, a place through which messages can be transmitted between agents and their controllers.

Parole. Recognition signal.

Quiet Ones. Homosexuals, used for homosexual entrapment and subsequent blackmail of anyone – male or female – upon whom the KGB want to exert pressure.

Rezident. The KGB local controller.

Rezidentura. The KGB organization within the embassy in any given country.

Referentura. That section of a Soviet embassy given over to KGB or GRU exclusive use. A *referentura* is banned to any ordinary diplomat. That includes the ambassador, if he is not a KGB man.

Roof. Legal cover for an illegal.

Ravens. Attractive men, used sexually to entrap any women whom the KGB wants to blackmail.

Swallows. Beautiful women, used sexually to entrap any man whom the KGB wishes to suborn by blackmail.

Swallows' Nest. A seduction apartment, especially equipped with cameras and audio recording equipment, to obtain incriminating, blackmailing material.

Safe House. A clandestine meeting place, either a house or an apartment, owned surreptitiously or through a cover by the Russians, where conferences can be held safe from rival intelligence interruption or where a person can be secreted.

Swim. For a KGB man to go from Russia on an assignment abroad.

Shoe. A false passport.

Shoemaker (or *cobbler*). The forger of that passport.

Split. To force a confession from someone.

Shavki. Literally scavenging mongrels, used disparagingly to describe small-time agents.

Stukachi. An informer.

Talent Spotter. An agent – frequently an agent of influence, sometimes a cut-out – whose function it is to recruit other spies.

Uncle. Term used by satellite intelligence services to describe their KGB overseers.

Walkers. People infiltrated across a border, extensively employed between East and West Germany.

Wet affairs. In Russian, *mokrie dela*. Assassinations.

Secret Security Organizations in Russia since 1917

1917	Vecheka
1922–3	GPU
1923–34	OGPU
1934–38	NKVD
1941–46	NKGB-NKVD
1946–53	MVD-MGB
1954–	KGB

Heads of the secret security organizations in Russia since 1917

1917–26	Dzerzhinsky
1926–34	Menzhinsky
1934–36	Yagoda
1936–38	Yezhov
1938–53	Beria
1954–58	Serov
1958–61	Shelepin
1961–67	Semichastny
1967–82	Andropov
1982–	Fedorchuk

BIBLIOGRAPHY

Allilluyeva, Svetlana. *Twenty Letters to a Friend*. Translated from the Russian by Priscilla Johnson. Hutchinson, London. 1967; Harper & Row, New York. 1967.

Amalrik, Andrei. *Will the Soviet Union Survive Until 1984?* Allen Lane, London. 1970; Harper & Row, New York. 1981.

Barron, John. *KGB: The Secret Work of Soviet Secret Agents*. Reader's Digest, New York. 1973; Hodder & Stoughton, London. 1974; Corgi, London. 1975.

Brown, Anthony Cave. *Bodyguard of Lies*. W. H. Allen, London. 1976; Bantam Books, New York. 1976; Star Books, London. 1977.

Bittman, Ladislav. *The Deception Game*. Syracuse, Syracuse University Research Corporation, New York. 1972.

Bierman, John. *Righteous Gentile: The Story of Raoul Wallenberg, Missing Hero of the Holocaust*. Viking, New York, 1981; Allen Lane, London. 1981.

Boyle, Andrew. *The Climate of Treason*. Hutchinson, London. 1979; Coronet Books, London. 1980; as *The Fourth Man*. Dial Press, New York. 1980; Bantam Books, New York, 1980.

Conquest, Robert. *The Great Terror: Stalin's Purges of the Thirties*. Macmillan, New York, 1968.

Conquest, Robert. *Kolyma: The Arctic Death Camps*. Macmillan, London. 1978; Viking Press, New York. 1978; Galaxy Books (OUP New York), New York. 1980.

Cookridge, E. H. *The Soviet Spy Net*. Frederick Muller Ltd., London. 1955. Under pseudonym 'E. H. Spiro'. *The Net That Covers the World*. Holt, Rinehart and Winston, New York. 1955.

Dallin, Alexander. *The Soviet Union and the United Nations*. Methuen & Co, London. 1962; Praeger, New York. 1962; Greenwood Press, London. 1976.

Epstein, Edward Jay. *Legend; The Secret World of Lee Harvey Oswald*. Reader's Digest, New York. 1978; Hutchinson, London. 1978; Arrow Books, Hutchinson. 1978.

Foote, Alexander. *Handbook for Spies*. London Museum Press, London. 1949; Doubleday, New York. 1949.

Franks, Lord. *Report on Official Secrets Act, London*. Her Majesty's Stationery Office, London. 1972.

Heilbrunn, Otto. *The Soviet Secret Services*. George Allen and Unwin, London. 1956; Praeger, New York. 1956.

Gouzenko, Igor. *The Iron Curtain*. Dutton, New York. 1948; as *This Was My Choice – Gouzenko's Story*. Eyre & Spottiswoode, London. 1948.

Hirsch, Richard. *The Soviet Spies*. Nicholas Kaye, London. 1947; Duell, New York. 1947.

Khrushchev, Nikita. *Khrushchev Remembers*. Translated from the Russian by Strobe Talbott. Andre Deutsch, London, 1971. Little, Brown, Boston. 1974.

Khokhlov, Nikolai. *In the Name of Conscience*. Translated from the Russian by Emily Kingsbery, McKay, New York. 1959; Frederick Muller, London. 1960.

Krivitsky, Walter. *I Was Stalin's Agent*. Hamish Hamilton. London. 1939; as *In Stalin's Secret Service*. Harper & Row, New York. 1939.

Leggett, George. *The Cheka: Lenin's Political Police*. Oxford University Press, Oxford and New York. 1981.

Newman, Bernard. *The Red Spider Web*. Latimer House, London. 1947.

Penkovsky, Oleg. *The Penkovsky Papers*. Translated from the Russian by P. Deriabin. Doubleday, New York. 1965; Collins, London. 1965.

Philby, Kim. *My Silent War*. McGibbon and Kee, London. 1968; Grove Press, New York. 1968; Panther, London. 1969.

Pincher, Chapman. *Their Trade Is Treachery*. Sidgwick & Jackson, London. 1981.

Report of the Royal Commission, Ottawa. Edmond Cloutier. 1946.

Report of the Royal Commission on Espionage, Commonwealth of Australia. Government Printer for New South Wales, Sydney, 1955.

Rositzke, Harry. *The KGB: The Eyes of Russia*. Doubleday, New York. 1981. Sidgwick & Jackson, London. 1982.

Seth, Ronald. *Forty Years of Soviet Spying*. Cassell, London. 1965; as *Unmasked: The Story of Soviet Espionage*. Hawthorn Books, New York. 1965.

Solzhenitsyn, Aleksandr. *The First Circle*. Translated from the Russian by Nicholas Bethell and David Burg. Farrar, Straus, New York. 1969.

Solzhenitsyn, Aleksandr. *The First Circle*. Translated from the Russian by Thomas Whitney. Harper & Row, New York. 1968; English translation by Michael Guybon. Harvill Press, London. 1968; Fontana, London. 1970.

Solzhenitsyn, Aleksandr. *One Day in the Life of Ivan Denisovich*. Translated by Max Hayward and Ronald Hingley. Praeger, New York. 1963; translated by Ralph Parker. Gollancz, London. 1963.

Solzhenitsyn, Aleksandr. *The Gulag Archipelago* (3 vols). Harvill Press, London. 1974–8; Harper, New York. 1974–8.

White, John Baker. *The Soviet Spy System*. The Falcon Press, London. 1948.

SOURCES

Note: to prevent the unnecessary repetition of U.S. Congressional committees and examining bodies I will follow the example of John Barron and substitute abbreviations:

SSIS – Subcommittee to Investigate the Administration of the Internal Security Act and other Internal Security Laws, Committee of the Judiciary, Senate.

HCUAA – House Committee of Un-American Activities.

H – Hearing.

R – Report to or from committee or sub-committee.

SS – Staff study.

Testimony of Nikolai Khokhlov. Activities of the Soviet Secret Service SSIS. H. 1954.

Exposé of Soviet Espionage. SSIS. R. 1960.

Testimony of Colonel Yevgeny Runge. SSIS. H. 5 February 1970.

Testimony of Ladislav Bittman. SSIS. H. 1971.

Testimony of Adam Joseph Galinski. HCUAA. H. 1960.

U.S.S.R. Labour Camps. SSIS. H. Parts 1 to 5. 1973.

Soviet Intelligence and Security Services. 1964–7. Selected Bibliography of Soviet Publications. SSIS. R. 1972.

Testimony of Frantisek Tisler. HCUAA. H. 1960.

Communist Psychological Warfare – Thought Control. HCUAA. H. 1958.

Religious Persecution in the U.S.S.R. HCUAA. 1968.

Soviet Covert Action. The Forgery Offensive. SSIS. H. 1980.

The Sverdlovsk Incident. SSIS. H. 1980.

Communist Bloc Activities in the U.S. Parts I and II. SSIS. H. 1975 and 1976.

Trotskyite Terrorist International. SSIS. H. 1975.

Surveillance Technology. SSIS. SS. 1975.

Organized Subversion in the U.S. Armed Forces. Part I. SSIS. SS. 1975.

Testimony of Captain Nikolai Fedorovich Artamonov. HCUAA. 1960.

INDEX

All Futura Books are available at your bookshop or newsagent, or can be ordered from the following address:
Futura Books, Cash Sales Department,
P.O. Box 11, Falmouth, Cornwall.

Please send cheque or postal order (no currency), and allow 45p for postage and packing for the first book plus 20p for the second book and 14p for each additional book ordered up to a maximum charge of £1.63 in U.K.

Customers in Eire and B.F.P.O. please allow 45p for the first book, 20p for the second book plus 14p per copy for the next 7 books, thereafter 8p per book.

Overseas customers please allow 75p for postage and packing for the first book and 21p per copy for each additional book.